the **24 sales traps** and how to avoid them

Recognizing the Pitfalls That Mislead Even the Best Performers

Dick Canada

AMACOM AMERICAN MANAGEMENT ASSOCIATION
New York • Atlanta • Chicago • Kansas City • San Francisco
Washington, D. C. • Brussels • Mexico City • Tokyo • Toronto

This publication is designed to provide accurate and authoritative information in regard to the subject matter covered. It is sold with the understanding that the publisher is not engaged in rendering legal, accounting, or other professional service. If legal advice or other expert assistance is required, the services of a competent professional person should be sought.

Library of Congress Cataloging-in-Publication Data

Canada, Dick, 1945–
    The 24 sales traps and how to avoid them : recognizing the pitfalls that
    mislead even the best performers / Dick Canada.
        p. cm.
    Includes index.
    ISBN 0-8144-7141-2 (pbk.)—0-8144-0735-8 (hc.)
        1. Selling. I. Title: Twenty four sales traps and how to avoid them. II. Title.

HF5438.25 .C28 2002
658.85--dc21

                                                            2001046414

Printing number

10 9 8 7 6 5 4 3 2 1

In loving memory of my parents,
Lawrence M. and Violet H. Canada

contents

preface

A wise person once said that you should begin a project with the end in mind. If that were the case, when you finished reading this book, this is what you would have learned: It is not what sales and marketing people don't know that is most likely to significantly hurt their performance; it is what they think they know that turns out to be either a partial truth, fallacy, or mistaken belief that affects their results more. We call these half-truths and falsehoods sales traps, and each trap springs from validated research. There are 24 traps that could be adversely affecting individual, team, group, and company sales performance. So much for the ending, let's go to the beginning.

MY FIRST SALES TRAP

It all began at the Xerox International Training Center (now known as Xerox Document University) in Leesburg, Virginia, where I was serving as a manager of training and development. Ted, a Xerox sales manager and a good friend of mine, stormed up to the table where I was having lunch with a few of our colleagues after a training session. The major account team Ted was in charge of was growing, and he was adding to his sales staff, but his new hires were not closing sales as effectively as he had hoped, and he was unhappy with

their lack of productivity. What's more, he couldn't see the benefit of pulling key staff out of the field to take the particular skill-
training course we were offering. He expected to see bottom-line
results in the field—and in his training expense budget—from our
sales training. I knew that he was dissatisfied with his team's performance. He had often complained about our skills-based training, saying, "They either have what it takes or they don't, so why
are we wasting our time training them?" This time, he was red-
hot angry.

And, inadvertently, I had just added fuel to the fire. Recently, we
had announced the results of a new sales research project conducted
by Xerox.[1] The study showed that without reinforcement, our
salespeople lost 87 percent of the sales skills they learned within
thirty days.

"So, now you're finally admitting that sales-skill training courses
don't work?" he asked, addressing me but looking around our table
with a triumphant smile on his face.

"Sales training doesn't work," I responded immediately, *"unless
sales managers are willing to reinforce it!"*

I didn't realize it at the time, but I had just identified my first sales
trap. What I mean by a sales trap is an incorrect action or strategy
undertaken by a salesperson or sales organization because of a mistaken belief, fallacy, or partial truth. The sales trap Ted had put his
finger on was "sales training doesn't work." This statement is a partial truth. In other words, taken at face value, it's true that sales training doesn't work because, as the Xerox study showed, attendees
forgot 87 percent of the skills they learned within thirty days. In
Ted's case, sales training didn't work because he (like many sales
managers) didn't reinforce the skills with his reps after the training
course was over. But what Ted said didn't go far enough. The sales
truth is "sales training doesn't work without reinforcement." Sales
traps are extremely important. They hurt an individual's performance and compensation and lower an organization's sales revenues

and margins. Salespeople should recognize and avoid these pitfalls and base their sales techniques on updated sales research.

SALES RESEARCH

Today we're in the fortunate position of being able to identify Sales Traps more accurately because of the revolutionary sales research done in the last twenty years. The scientific validation of sales principles and techniques has introduced standards of measurement, control, and uniformity to the sales cycle and has introduced professionalism to the sales training process that was unheard of before.

The 24 Sales Traps and How to Avoid Them relies on this published research—as well as field research conducted by The Dartmouth Group, Ltd., and the Institute for Global Sales Studies—to establish that key ideas and beliefs about sales are based on incorrect information. It also includes real-life examples and practical information from savvy and experienced sales professionals.

WHO THIS BOOK IS FOR

I've come to see that given the choice between sales traps and sales truths, salespeople choose the sales truths. They choose the more effective way to sell, if for no other reason than that the correct way enables them to work smarter—not harder—with the same or better bottom-line results. Of course, you'll still have to work hard. But you're already doing that, or you wouldn't have picked up this book.

This book is for you if you:

△ Are searching for easier access to the approaches and techniques that improve sales effectiveness

△ Are curious about the process of selling and want to do it better

△ Have ever thought that "this is the way we've always done it" wasn't a good enough answer

△ Have known on a gut level that the techniques you learned didn't seem right, but weren't sure of what to do instead

△ Have ever wanted to know the valid reasons for sales principles and techniques, beyond the reasons you hear so often

This book is designed to be useful to:

△ Salespeople at all levels of expertise

△ Sales managers, trainers, and coaches

△ Consultants

△ People who want to get others to think differently

△ Managers, trainers, and coaches

△ Students considering a career in consultative sales or marketing

This book will help you not only to identify what you've been doing wrong, but also to replace your mistakes with the right technique for the right circumstance. Above all, this book will show you how to improve your sales effectiveness.

acknowledgments

I'd like to thank the dean of the Kelley School of Business, Dr. Dan Dalton, and the chairman of the marketing department, Dr. Frank Acito. Both were encouraging and supportive of our efforts to raise money to establish the Institute for Global Sales Studies. I would also like to thank Dr. Rosann Spiro, former chairperson of the American Marketing Association. Not only has she challenged me, but she has also helped me immensely in deciding what academic research might be helpful to this book. I would also like to recognize Dr. John Summers, Dr. Gil Frisbie, Dr. Tom Hustadt, Dr. Ron Stephenson, Dr. Rockney Walters, Dr. Ray Burke, Dr. Dan Smith, and Brenda Crohn, who have lent their moral and intellectual support to the endeavors of the Institute for Global Sales Studies. Without their support, the research that forms the basis of this book might never have been completed.

Without my colleagues and partners at The Dartmouth Group, Ltd., this book would not have been as comprehensive. Therefore, my thanks to Susan Woods, whose loyalty and support has been the best. Also, my gratitude to R. Michael Lockman; his input and suggestions for this final manuscript were insightful and helpful. My appreciation also extends to Mike Navel, who has the uncanny knack of being able to take complex problems and discussions and reduce them to a simple and understandable format. You have a gift. I need to recognize Tricia Wilson for her constructive input; her passion for consulting and training makes The Dartmouth Group, Ltd., a fun place to work. Lastly, my gratitude to Tracy Welch for her behavior analysis studies during client field observations, Flora Walters for her administrative support with this manuscript, and Erika Meditz for initial editing.

I would like to document my thanks and appreciation to two colleagues in the sales profession who have inspired, motivated, and mentored me over the last two decades through their books, their articles, their research, and their friendship: Neil Rackham and Dr. Richard Ruff. It's now possible to validate sales techniques, thanks to researchers such as Neil Rackham, Dr. Richard Ruff, Robert B. Miller and Stephen E. Heiman (authors of *The New Conceptual Selling and Strategic Selling*), Dr. Rosann L. Spiro, Dr. Thomas N. Ingram, Dr. Ramon A. Avila, Dr. Ronald E. Michaels, Dr. Barton A. Weitz, Dr. Charles M. Futrell, Professor Tom Leigh, Dr. Dan McQuiston, Jamie Comstock and Gary Higgins, Lawrence G. Friedman and Timothy R. Furey (authors of *The Channel Advantage*), and Jerome A. Colletti (author of *Compensating New Sales Roles*), to name only a few. Because of their work, we can now give definitive answers to a myriad of questions about sales principles and techniques.

I would also like to mention some key people who over the years have kept my passion for sales, consulting, training, and teaching burning: Carole Canada Driver, Jim Cotterill, Jack Fidger, Bernie Sanders, Larry Thomas, Don Kutch, and Karen Thor. Additional mention goes to those sales practitioners, many of whom I worked with at Procter & Gamble and Xerox, who have affected my thinking regarding the sales profession: Ted Rubley, Jon King, Bridget Momcilovich, Jim Rayl, Jack Thompson, Greg Graham, C. Bruce

McIntyre, William G. Mays, George C. Platt, David V. LeVine, J. J. Moffat, Tom Palmer, Frank Pacetta, Thomas M. O'Neil, Sue Matchett, John Cuny, John Pitz, Mark D. Slaby, Gina Shupe, Jay Preston, David Renzi, Mary Riley Quinn, Jon Robisch, Paul MacKinnon, Jim Piotter, Pat Elizondo, Ross Raifsnider, Bill Ziegert, Steve Iden, Jim Wallace, Jason Craven, Kristi Johnson, Jennifer Brase, Mark Lindenberg, Judy Paton Schnettgoecke, Jeff Henry, and Suzy Yancey DuBois, Greg Kluesner, Phil Engle, Dave Pannell, and Rich Schwimmer.

To those worthy competitors from IBM during the 1970s, thanks for the defeats, and a few victories, to Bob Armstrong, David Knoll, and Joe Galati.

I would like to thank those clients who have unselfishly participated in our research efforts to either confirm or deny the validity of many of the traps included in this book. For those clients that I failed to mention, please accept my heartfelt apologies for the oversight. Our sincere appreciation is extended to Greg Lucas, Larry O'Connor, Greg Lucas, Gerald Rush, Ben Campbell, Tom Bareford, Marsha Jay, Jill Hill, Chip Myers, Gilmour Lake, Mike O'Connor, Randy McNutt, Shelby Solomon, Channing Mitzell, Vicki Mech Hester, Ed. D., Jane Ellis, Don Schenkel, Dr. Jack Engledow, and Ed Engledow.

I would be remiss if I didn't recognize my friend Dr. Ed. Mitchell, one of the best listeners and communicators I have ever known, for his insights into people.

A special thanks to Russell P. Valentine, M.D., whose professional counsel and friendship I greatly appreciate—and this generation's answer to Marcus Welby, M.D. Thanks, Russ, for helping me to be here to write this book.

I wish I could individually thank each of the marketing students who over the years have taken my consultative marketing and sales management classes at the Kelley School of Business at Indiana University. Not only have they participated in my classroom research projects and lent support to the Institute for Global Sales Studies, they have also participated in my "experimental groups" so that I could test various "half-baked" consultative models in the hopes that these ideas would become "fully baked." I will be forever grateful. Please continue to stay in touch.

I would not have finished this book without my literary agent, Martha Jewett *(www.marthajewett.com)*. Thanks, Martha, for your immense help and your solid writing and editorial consultation, as well as your excellent literary representation. You are a true professional and no-nonsense person. Smith College should be proud of you.

Nor would this book have been published without the support of my editor, Ellen Kadin, at AMACOM Books. Thanks, Ellen, for recognizing how this book was different from the other sales and consulting books. And to Christina McLaughlin for her fine editing skills and suggestions that made this book better. You were truly impressive, Christina.

Next to last, my special recognition to Frank and Bets Johnson for your love and support over the years. I love you both. Also, to the quintessential family patriarch and matriarch, Joe and Bev Cegala, you have affected me more than you'll ever know. And to Jenny, Vince, and David, may you live your dreams.

Last, my heartfelt love goes out to my wonderful wife, Debbie, the best of the best, for her understanding and patience as I continued to sand the rough edges of this book—often past the midnight hour. And, of course, my two lovely daughters, Andria and Erin. I love each of you more as the days pass.

Sales Trap *n*: An incorrect action or strategy undertaken by a salesperson or sales organization because of a mistaken belief, fallacy, or partial truth.

the **24 sales traps** and how to avoid them

what you think you know

SALES TRAPS result from three things: fallacies, mistaken beliefs, and partial truths. In selling, it's easy to believe the wrong thing and as a consequence do the wrong thing. A fallacy is a false or erroneous idea that is the result of having the *wrong information* or making the *wrong inference*. Mistaken beliefs that cause people to fall into sales traps include cultural stereotypes and prejudices. For example, a mistaken belief based upon a stereotype is that top salespeople need to be aggressive. Scientific research has proved that a salesperson does not have to be aggressive to succeed.

Sales traps can also result from having the wrong information or from applying the right information in the wrong situation. For example, your information about the competitive marketplace may be outdated. You may not be aware of validated, effective sales strategies or the latest sales research. The information at your disposal may be incomplete or unavailable. You may not bring back enough information about client needs. In addition, a fallacy can also occur when you apply the correct information in the wrong circumstances. For example, a transactional sales strategy, such as increasing sales activity, may be mistakenly chosen in a consultative sales situation. (See Sales Trap 20, "If You Generate Sales Activity, You'll Close More Sales.") Having the wrong information leads to poor results for reasons that you can't see or don't acknowledge.

You can also fall into a sales trap if you draw the wrong conclusion from the information at hand. You may have correct information or information that is good enough for your sales purpose, but make the wrong inference from it, resulting in a fallacy. For example, Sales Trap 21, "Top Performers Are the Best Teachers," is the result of a fallacy. In this case, the inference is that because top performers are the best at what they do, they will be the best at teaching others what they do. But, in fact, top performers aren't sure why they are the best. Finally, partial truths can result in sales traps. For example, it is often said that salespeople should ask questions in order to persuade someone to do something. Well, yes, but that is only a partial truth. Salespeople should probe to understand the customer *first*, and try to persuade *second*.

WHY AVOID SALES TRAPS?

The 24 sales traps are illustrations of ways in which salespeople, sales managers, consultants, and sales organizations *do the wrong thing* and how this prevents them from achieving high-performance results. Sales traps have serious consequences. For instance, one trap says that sales-skill training works. This is partially true; however, sales-skill training doesn't work without coaching and reinforcement. In life, we can usually get by without holding or acting on the correct belief or having the best information. But what if doing the wrong thing as a result of believing the wrong thing makes a big difference? In sales, doing the wrong thing can lead to a negative outcome with serious financial consequences. It may mean not making the sale. It may even mean losing a large client or a favorite customer.

And what if the sales trap is so seductive or so deeply ingrained in a salesperson's thinking that it becomes an unconscious pattern, a bad habit? In the worst case, you may have fallen into a sales trap and not even realized it. How do you know where you need to make improvements if you think what you're doing is just fine?

How do you know where to start?

FOCUS ON THE 20 PERCENT YOU DO *WRONG*

The 24 sales traps show you how to stop doing the things you do that are wrong and replace them with what's correct. You've all heard of the 80/20 rule. It's used almost as commonly as Catch-22. If you're a sales manager, for example, you probably can identify the 20 percent of your accounts that produce 80 percent of your sales and the 20 percent of your sales reps that produce 80 percent of your sales revenues.

THE 80/20 RULE. The 80/20 rule says that a selected small fraction *in terms of number* almost always accounts for a large fraction in terms of effect. If you can identify which 20 percent produces the much larger effect, then you can take steps that focus on that 20 percent and benefit from the much larger effect that the 20 percent produces. *It is not what sales and marketing people don't know that is most likely to significantly hurt their performance; it is what they think they know that turns out to be either a partial truth, a fallacy, or a mistaken belief that affects their results more.*

WHICH 20 PERCENT IS WRONG? I can't say with scientific certainty that 20 percent of what salespeople do is wrong, but my experience in training and consulting tells me that the 80/20 rule comes close. Salespeople do the right thing about 80 percent of the time. But approximately 20 percent of the time, they don't. What's more, most salespeople don't even know what exactly they're doing wrong.

For instance, if a salesperson believes he gets too many objections, he probably will want to study objection-handling techniques. But one research finding has revealed that objections are often symptoms of a bigger problem, such as ineffective probing. In this case, the salesperson believes the problem is one thing (objections), when it is really another (probing).

As another example, many salespeople believe that open-ended questions are more effective than closed-ended questions. These salespeople don't know that it isn't the category of questions that matters; the type of question within each category is more important.

SELECTION CRITERIA FOR SALES TRAPS

No one—including academics, consultants, and senior managers—is immune from sales traps. There may well be more than just 24 of them. The ones I've identified here meet the following two stringent criteria:

1. The sales trap will have a large negative impact on business results if it is not immediately recognized and avoided. (Negative results include financial loss, lack of customer loyalty and retention, and strategic market competitiveness issues.)

2. There is reliable published or field research with which to refute the mistaken beliefs, fallacies, or partial truths inherent in the sales trap.

If there wasn't sound evidence to prove that a belief was a sales trap, I didn't include it.

BENEFITS OF AVOIDING THE 24 SALES TRAPS. If you avoid the 24 sales traps and execute the action points, you're going to see a dramatic increase in your personal sales effectiveness and sales results (remember the 80/20 ratio). If your organization avoids these traps consistently across the board, it will be on its way to being a successful sales team.

Avoiding the 24 sales traps will enable you to:

Δ Increase your sales call effectiveness

Δ Improve your personal selling skills

Δ Have a greater impact on your buyer's business

Δ Improve your customer retention and customer satisfaction

Δ Be more effective in sales management

Δ Produce higher sales revenues and profits for your company and for your clients

HOW TO USE THIS BOOK

This book identifies six basic principles followed by successful sales organizations. These principles are based on ten years of observation of top companies, teams, and individual sales forces. Avoiding the sales traps associated with each principle will help you achieve success in that area. For each sales trap, you'll find explanatory text, action points, and, at the end of each sales trap, the "sales truth," the counterintuitive sales reality. The sales truths summarize published and field research, as well as best practices. The action points I give for each sales trap are practical real-world guidelines based on the best practices of The Dartmouth Group, the Institute for Global Sales Studies at Indiana University, and hundreds of top-notch companies.

Endnotes with full citations are given at end of the book. See the notes section for more information on the research and/or researcher who disproves each mistaken belief, fallacy, or half-truth.

It includes primary sources, secondary sources, and other research material (including field studies and face-to-face interviews). The names in the case studies and examples have been changed to protect confidentiality.

I've designed this book to be engaging and fun (well, as engaging and fun as any sales book can be). Skim the table of contents, and identify the sales traps that make you go "Hmmm" or that you disagree with. Turn to the sales truth at the end of each. Do you agree with it? Did you get it? If you didn't get it, or you don't believe it, you'll want to read the explanation. If you know the answer, but you want to see how I came up with it, you may want to read the explanation to see why your answer is correct.

THE SIX PRINCIPLES OF LEADING SALES ORGANIZATIONS

In order to place the sales traps in this book in their real-world context, I've organized them around the six key principles that leading sales organizations, teams, and top performers follow. These are the six principles that differentiate average-performing groups and salespeople from those that are outstanding. Companies such as Xerox, IBM, Dell Computer, Microsoft, Procter & Gamble, General Electric, Guidant, Motorola, Eli Lilly, INB Bank of Indiana (now Bank One), Duracell, Hewlett-Packard, Thomson RCA, Northwestern Mutual, UPS, and AT&T espouse these six principles:

1. Focus outside.

2. Get the most out of the best people.

3. Train effectively.

4. Create value.

5. Offer feedback and opportunities for learning.

6. Use the Internet and databases effectively.

Fundamentally, these six principles incorporate the 24 sales truths. The trick is to identify and avoid the sales traps in order to improve your performance—company, team, or individual.

LEARNING SALES EFFECTIVENESS. Every week I am asked some version of the question, "What am I doing wrong?" Specifically, I'm asked the following three questions every week by salespeople:

1. What am I (is our team, our department, our organization, our company) doing wrong—so that I (we) can stop doing it?

2. What am I (is our organization) doing right—so that I (we) can continue doing it and improve upon it?

3. How do I (we) know what's correct—based on the research, not just an opinion?

The goal of *The 24 Sales Traps and How to Avoid Them* is to answer these questions. If you want to see results, you need to fix your mistakes. Start by avoiding the 24 sales traps in this book. *The 24 Sales Traps and How to Avoid Them* puts a counterintuitive emphasis on *what salespeople do wrong* because in sales, especially at advanced levels, there are so many ways to do things right. There are many fewer ways to do things wrong.

Finally, if this book does nothing else, I hope it causes you to see your "sales piece" differently, to see what you've been doing in a new light, so that you can be more effective. The reason to change your behavior based on the sales truths is simple: They work. In sales, actions based on fallacies, mistaken beliefs, and half-truths don't work. When salespeople believe and do the wrong thing, they often fall into one or more of these 24 sales traps.

adopt an outside focus

SUCCESSFUL sales teams focus their energies outside the company. The efforts of sales and marketing appear seamless; they appear to be one entity, not two, when solving customer needs.

CUSTOMERS COME FIRST

Leading sales teams focus on customers' buying preferences, requirements, and needs before focusing on their own targets. They place their focus *outside* of their organizations by following their customers' buying trends. Less stellar sales organizations focus inside their organizations and then figure out how to capture the customers. For example, people in these less stellar organizations place more emphasis on internal paperwork to cover their behinds than on quickly and effectively solving customer issues. In contrast, sales leaders make their customers' requirements and needs their priority, then align their sales and marketing operations and processes to best address those needs.

For example, Dell Computer Corporation stays abreast with—if not ahead of—the buying requirements and patterns of its customers. Michael Dell recognized in the early 1980s that his targeted customer base didn't see the value of a faster processor. He changed strategic direction from creating faster processors to making computers available over the phone. He recognized that there were many customers who were knowledgeable enough to order their computer solutions directly from Dell over the phone (and eventually over the Net). Thus, Dell has become a giant by focusing on what it *knows* its customers want and aligning the company to meet those requirements, rather than focusing on what it *thinks* its customers want.

Sales forces should focus on solutions, not on particular products. When products that are needed to solve key customer problems do not exist and must be developed, the products should be developed by the marketing departments *but in concert with the customers.*

FOCUS ON SOLUTIONS

Salespeople should focus much more heavily on product *solutions* than on *features and advantages.* An excellent example of this is IBM's sales force, because it focuses on solutions and not on pushing products. Likewise, Xerox's salespeople thoroughly probe to understand the customer's needs today and in the future before they talk about new products, new features, new pricing on old products, and so on. Such salespeople are "walking problem solvers" rather than "talking brochures."

CLOSE COORDINATION OF MARKETING AND SALES

What is usually a broad chasm between the marketing department and the sales organization is narrow in top sales organizations. The right hand should know what the left hand is doing, and why. Both groups should focus on the customer and coordinate their activities to provide the best solutions for the customer—even if they have to create solutions "on the fly" to satisfy customer needs. They should work closely together to develop solutions, attractive pricing, and customer incentives.

One of the key factors that reduced this gap between sales and marketing in the 1980s was the "quality initiatives." The companies that did a good job of implementing a strong quality program tended to end up with a strong sense of cooperation between sales and marketing. This makes sense, given that the primary goal of quality programs was to figure out how to focus better on the customer.

Xerox Corporation, which in 1989 won the Malcolm Baldrige Award, presented by the U.S. Department of Commerce to companies that exemplify the best in American business, for its Leadership Through Quality Program, is an example of a company that attained a close working relationship between sales and marketing. As Scott Bradley, a vice president at Xerox, said, "Our quality program really helps us to focus on the customer requirements, both external and internal, in order to make certain that we are creating customer value. And, one of the keys for us is when our marketing and sales organizations work closely together."[1]

Xerox was by no means the only company to effectively coordinate sales and marketing activities. Procter & Gamble used a team selling approach to literally force cooperation between marketing and sales by including people from brand marketing and sales, and also key management personnel, on the sales teams that work with megachains such as Kroger, Wal-Mart, and Target. Salespeople who fail to keep their focus on the customer begin to fall into sales traps. They become too aggressive, fail to relate the product to the customer's needs, and fail to recognize potential champions.

*   *   *

> ## sales trap 1:
> ## You Must Be Aggressive to Succeed in Sales

Here's the idea: You have to be aggressive to succeed in sales.

This mistaken belief is widely held. But when salespeople believe they need to be aggressive, and when they are aggressive, they focus on the wrong thing: themselves. Aggressiveness *reduces* sales effectiveness because it reduces what should be your outside focus on the customer.

THE CULTURAL STEREOTYPE OF THE OBNOXIOUS SALESPERSON

Everyone recognizes the cultural stereotype of the obnoxious salesperson. At the beginning of each semester in the class I teach on sales management and consultative marketing, I ask my students to raise their hands if they want to be salespeople. Although the thirty to forty students who have registered for the class clearly know that they're taking a career-oriented sales class, only about three in ten students will raise his or her hand.

"Why is it that you wouldn't want to pursue a sales career?" I then ask the others.

"I don't want to be obnoxious" is the most common answer.

These students don't want to be salespeople because they think salespeople have to be aggressive or—worse yet—obnoxious if they are to succeed. Some students tone their answers down and say they don't feel it's in their nature to be as "persistent" or to "bug" customers as much as they think they will have to. (Persistence is an important ingredient in sales success, as I discuss shortly.)

The idea that you have to be aggressive in order to succeed in sales is practically universal. Corporate recruiters report that in recruiting interviews, students mention their aggressiveness as a positive attribute that will lead to their success on the job. However, the recruiters aren't necessarily looking for aggressiveness, because it is not tied to sales success.

Is there a rational foundation for students' aversion to salespeople? Unfortunately, yes. In the real world, we've all dealt with obnoxious salespeople. "Pressuring the customer succeeds in very small sales or with very unsophisticated buyers. But in larger sales and with sophisticated customers, the effect of pressure is negative— aggressive selling hurts your sales results," says Neil Rackham.[2]

AN EXAMPLE OF AN AGGRESSIVE SALESPERSON

An encounter with an aggressive, dominant, controlling salesperson might look like the following scenario, in which Debbie Dale is exploring her options for a cellular phone. The dialogue goes something like this:

Phone Man (PM): May I help you?

Debbie Dale (DD): Well, I'm looking for an inexpensive cellular phone.

PM: Good. You have come to the right place. Are you looking for any particular features?

DD: I thought I might like to have voice mail and call waiting, if those features don't cost me too much.

PM: No sweat. Our pricing is as competitive as anybody's. Let's look at several models we have here. Were you interested in activating the phone today?

DD: I don't know. I'm just looking at different options right now.

PM: Well, no need to look any further. We have everything you need. Will you be paying by credit card or check?

DD: Oh, I seem to have forgotten my purse. I'm sorry. Bye.

Debbie was actually thinking, but was too polite to say, "Neither, sir; I'm giving my money to one of your competitors." We have all had unproductive exchanges with obnoxious salespeople. Salespeople who believe they need to be aggressive in order to succeed in sales put *themselves* first and the customer second. Debbie's needs were secondary to the salesperson's need to close, or perhaps, worse still, to his company's need for the order.

Fortunately, however, a salesperson does not have to be aggressive or obnoxious in order to succeed. As a matter of fact, aggressiveness is an undesirable trait.

AGGRESSIVE SALESPEOPLE TURN BUYERS OFF

It's a shame that so many salespeople are aggressive. Customers consider salespeople to be guilty of being aggressive until proven innocent. At the very least, customers consider them to be guilty of not always putting the customer's needs ahead of their own. Aggressiveness doesn't bring credibility to the profession. Unlike assertiveness, hard work, or ambition, all of which help in sales as much as in any career, aggressiveness gives the sales profession a bad name.

Research shows that aggressive salespeople turn buyers off. Buyers rank dominance as one of the least preferred qualities in salespeople. Instead, they want salespeople who are confident and assertive. Dominance is viewed as self-oriented, not customer-oriented, and therefore reduces buyer trust.[3]

A BETTER EXAMPLE TO FOLLOW

Here's how a more confident and less aggressive salesperson would have handled the sales interaction with Debbie:

PM: May I help you?

DD: Well, I'm looking for an inexpensive cellular phone.

PM: Good. Can you tell me what price range you were looking at?

DD: Oh, around $75.

PM: I see. Any particular features you were looking for?

DD: I thought I might like to have voice mail and call waiting, if those particular features don't cost too much.

PM: Normally not. But the price may or may not seem like a lot to you, depending on the particular needs that you have. Do you mind if I ask you a few questions in order to help identify what we might be able to offer as a possible solution to your problem?

DD: Okay. What do you want to know?

PM: Well, to begin with, how much time do you expect to be on your phone each day?

This salesperson put the customer first, probing in depth by asking appropriate questions, and displaying genuine concern for Debbie.

Channing (Chap) Mitzell, president of the Windsor Financial Group, Ltd., put it best when he said, "The era of the pushy, aggressive financial consultant and their organizations putting their own quotas, requirements, and needs before their client's needs is over. In our industry, if a consultant doesn't view value from the customer perspective, they won't last to view value from their own perspective."

ACTION POINTS

→ *Being aggressive may get you the appointment, but it won't get you the sale (and it definitely won't get you the sustainable business relationship).* Buyers prefer sellers whose personal style is cooperative, not aggressive. The cooperative style is characterized by the salesperson's receptivity, precision, friendliness, and lack of contentiousness. Buyers don't like salespeople who compete with them.[4]

→ *Be professional.* Above everything else, clients want a professional relationship, and they want salespeople who are trustworthy, composed, and task-oriented.[5]

→ *Display concern about the customer.* The best way to show concern is to ask questions. It is difficult to be aggressive if you are asking lots of good questions. And it's always better to show concern for the customer than to talk about how wonderful your product or service is.[6]

SALES TRUTH 1: Buyers don't like salespeople who are aggressive.

---

sales trap 2:
You Can Make a Complex Sale Without an Account Champion

It's a mistake to believe that you can make a complex sale without a "champion" inside the account—a person who wants to see you make the sale and is willing to help you do so. Research shows that complex sales can't be made without such help.[7] Large corporations may have decentralized corporate structures, no clear purchasing channel, and an enormous number of people involved. This makes finding the key players in the buyer's decision-making process maddeningly difficult, expensive, and sometimes nearly impossible. It's difficult to focus outside, on the customer, under such circumstances. And yet many try.

WHAT HAPPENS WITHOUT AN ACCOUNT CHAMPION
Here's a common scenario:

> Heather, a three-year sales veteran for the Atlantic Storm & Casualty Company, knew a lot of people at Global Enterprises, a potentially large account. Heather knew decision makers, decision influencers, policy administrators, receptionists, and even the window cleaner. Heather had been working with the key personnel at Global for fourteen months. They had been receptive in meetings to her ideas regarding additional coverages for their offices along the Atlantic and Pacific seaboards, which were often hit by hurricanes, violent storms, and earthquakes, not to mention floods and heavy snow damage.
>
> She had displayed concern for her customer. She had probed effectively and thoroughly to understand her client's needs. Her prices were competitive, and Global's

people liked her. But Heather couldn't secure the business relationship. She finally convinced herself that these nice people at Global were indecisive and fearful of making decisions. How else could they like her and need her policies, but still not move forward with business?

Unfortunately, this story is all too common—for both parties. It's frustrating to the salesperson or consultant who has invested her or his time with an account, but can't seem to advance the account far enough to get an order. And it's frustrating to the people at the account to invest their time in meetings that end without any definite progress. What's wrong? Although Heather knew many key people, she didn't have an internal champion inside the account. Rather than investing all her time in developing superficial relationships, she should have focused more of her energies on finding and maintaining an account champion.

THE INTRICACIES INSIDE THE ACCOUNT

In *Strategic Selling*, Robert Miller and Stephen Heiman reveal that top-performing salespeople have internal "coaches" who, among other things, help guide the salespeople over, under, and around the various political sensitivities and hidden agendas within the account.[8] In Miller and Heiman's terminology, *coach* means "internal account champion." Later, I will use the term *coach* to refer to the role the sales manager or an outside trainer undertakes when he or she teaches a sales rep or gives one-on-one feedback about sales skills. Therefore, for the sake of clarity, in this discussion I will use *internal champion* instead of Miller and Heiman's word *coach*.[9]

The internal champion functions as an "inside salesperson" for the "outside salesperson." In other words, when the salesperson isn't at the account and when closed-door meetings take place, the salesperson's internal champion can go to bat to support the sale. In some cases, the internal champion will even sell the outside salesperson's ideas, opinions, and solutions to the key people in his or her own organization.[10]

Understanding the political issues and recognizing the sacred cows within an account is just another key element in an outside focus that puts the customer first. Corporate cultures breed sensitivities and strong opinions, and salespeople have to have an inside track in order to understand these issues and therefore to sell effectively. Today's salespeople need to send the message that they care enough to understand the client's behind-the-scenes concerns. Because complex sales involve multiple players with various perspectives, an internal champion is necessary if the salesperson is to navigate the corridors and unlock doors throughout the account.

WAYS THE INTERNAL CHAMPION HELPS

Returning to the scenario with Heather, let's see how having an internal champion might have helped. If Heather had taken the time to identify, select, and ask for the help of an internal champion, she might have secured the business relationship and cut her sales cycle in half. And she might also have reduced the frustration level of certain people within the account who felt that she wasn't making progress.

The internal champion could have advised Heather that the president of his company had been a college roommate of the senior vice president of sales for Heather's competitor. This might have led Heather to use a different strategy. For example, she could have suggested that her company did not expect to replace the competitor's business, but would merely supplement it. That way, Heather wouldn't have been a threat to the relationship between Global's president and his college friend.

This inside information would have also reduced the anxiety level of people at Global who reported to the president and knew of his relationship with her competitor's senior manager. While there is rarely such a thing as just one decision maker in a complex sale, there is almost always an internal champion who can help make an affirmative decision a little bit easier.

HOW TO IDENTIFY AN INTERNAL CHAMPION
The following steps will help you to identify your internal champion:

1. *Find decision influencers and decision makers.* List the key decision influencers (people who do not have the final say but will influence the decision outcome) and decision makers (the people who will take the responsibility for making the decision).

2. *Determine which of the decision influencers and decision makers will help you.* Seek out their colleagues' perceptions of these potential internal champions. When seeking perceptions, you are trying to get answers to such questions as, Which of the people within the company might be willing to help? Which ones can you trust? Which ones have the power but maybe not the position? Which ones' ideas would be more likely to align with your own philosophy of business? Which ones are destined for promotion?

3. *Ask for introductions.* If you don't already know one or more of these potential internal champions, you might ask someone in the account that you do know if he or she would be kind enough to introduce you.

4. *Meet.* Try to secure a thirty-minute initial meeting with the potential internal champion to assess how you might work with her or him. This internal champion can also advise you on your sales strategy and offer advice and counsel concerning the best plan for developing a partnership between your organization and the client's.

5. *Ask the person if he or she will function as your internal champion.* Ask the individual to help you, so that you can be the most effective not only for yourself and your company, but also for the account. Explain that his or her suggestions and counsel will not only help you to avoid potential land mines but also help you to create better value for the champion's company by enabling you to understand its inner workings more fully.

ACTION POINTS

→ *You can't do it by yourself.* Research shows that to make complex sales, you need to have an internal champion.

→ *Maintain two-way communication with your internal champion.* Make an agreement with your internal champion to keep each other apprised of the efforts each of you is making.

→ *Don't become too dependent on one account champion.* A note of caution here: People in organizations change. They retire, they're replaced, they're promoted, and they fall out of favor. Be careful not to place all your eggs in one basket with just one internal champion. The more perspectives and insights that you can get into the inner workings of an account, the better—for both parties.

SALES TRUTH 2: In complex selling, you need an internal champion.

> sales trap 3:
> ## It's Best to Offer Solutions to Problems You See

As a general rule, it's good to offer solutions to customer problems.

True or false?

If you say "true," you're like a lot of salespeople I know.

But you're wrong.

It's a mistake to assume that you should offer solutions to customer problems that you see. Contrary to the conventional wisdom, it's generally not a good idea to offer your solutions to customer problems unless the customer recognizes these problems.[11] The fallacy is that if we can help customers understand their problems clearly enough—if we're persuasive enough as salespeople—then they'll buy what we're selling. But this doesn't always work. Moreover, like Sales Traps 1 and 2, this trap causes the salesperson to focus on himself or herself and not on the customer, which results in fewer successful sales.

TRYING TO GET THE BUYER TO SEE A PROBLEM

Consider the following example in which the buyer doesn't see a problem as being big enough to solve. How does the consultant react? In this dialogue, Joe is a consultant selling advertising services. Bev, the customer, is the vice president (VP) of marketing at a major corporation:

Joe (consultant): What ad agency do you presently use?

Bev (VP of marketing): Gloom, Gloomier, & Gloomiest in New York.

Joe: Are you happy with their ad campaigns?

Bev: Not necessarily. They don't seem to generate as much business as we would like.

Joe: That is too bad. But we will be able to help you there. Our ad campaigns are likely to increase your sales here at Optimism, Ltd.

Bev: Well, they might do that. But we're not ready to change ad agencies just yet. Our problem with Gloom is not serious enough for us to change agencies at this point. It's true that one ad campaign that we selected from Gloom didn't perform as well as we had hoped. But, hey, Joe, those things happen. We have been with Gloom for thirteen years now. Besides, we may have an image problem—at least according to one of our clients.

Joe: I understand, Bev. We could really help you there. One of our core competencies is conducting ad and PR campaigns to improve a company's image.

Bev: Hold on, Joe. I know you could probably solve that problem. But it's really not big enough for us to sweat that either, and we aren't willing to go through the hassle of changing agencies. Remember, only one of our clients seems concerned about our image. The rest of them, about 99 percent, think our image is great. Why don't I call you when we are ready to change agencies? Thanks for stopping by, though, Joe. We may be in touch.

Joe kept trying to sell his solution to what he perceived was the customer's problem without listening to the customer. He didn't want to hear that Bev didn't think the problem was big enough to solve, and he lost the sale. By probing more effectively, Joe might have saved the sale. He could have explored the consequences of the problem (and perhaps led Bev to see it as more serious) or explored other problems that might be a reason for a change of agencies.

BUYER RESISTANCE

Research shows that people buy when the pain of making a change is less than the pain of staying the same.[12] In other words, buyers need to see the problem as being big enough to justify their going through the hassle of solving it.

A buyer may not be ready to acknowledge a problem. What seems to you to be a serious problem may not be perceived as serious by the buyer. A good example from outside the sales arena is the married couple whose marital problems appear to the outside world to be serious enough to make the couple a likely candidate for divorce. Yet they do not get divorced because the hassle, risk, and financial cost of divorce as they *perceive them* are not offset by the size of the problems in their marriage. In other words, people differ in how they will adjust to, adapt to, and live with their problems.

It is helpful for salespeople to separate customer problems into two categories: problems that the customer is willing to live with and problems that the customer wants to solve. Customers are more receptive to the solutions you offer when they perceive their problems as serious enough to solve.

Returning to the initial scenario with Bev and Joe, a buyer may agree that a problem exists, but not think it's serious enough to solve, especially if there is a substantial risk associated with the solution. A buyer also may not see that a problem exists, even though one does. The solution here is to either probe the buyer for problems or conduct your due diligence efforts with other people who may be more familiar with the problems than the buyer. A buyer may also see that a problem exists, want to solve it, and already be looking around for potential solutions. Let's revisit the scenario with Bev and Joe and consider two of these situations.

EXAMPLE 1. THE CUSTOMER DOESN'T PERCEIVE A PROBLEM, BUT ONE EXISTS

Joe: Are you confident that you are projecting the right image?

Bev: (She doesn't see that a problem exists.) I think so, Joe.

Joe: (He recognizes that Bev may not realize that she has a problem.) Are you comfortable that your current image will still be attractive to your targeted customers three to five years from now?

Bev: What do you mean?

Joe: Buying patterns of customers are continually changing. You may want to have the image of your company stay abreast of these changes, such as lower prices and purchasing convenience. It often takes a company two or three years to change its image. That's why I was wondering if that could be a potential problem.

Bev: Well, put that way, Joe, it might be. Tell me more.

Joe: Before I can explain much more, I need to ask you a few questions about your current image, your current targeted customers, and what changes you anticipate in your company and your customers three to five years from now. Would that be okay?

Bev: Yes.

Joe: For instance, how would you describe the image that you want your customers to have of Optimist?

Bev: Excellent question. Let's see, . . .

EXAMPLE 2: THE CUSTOMER RECOGNIZES THE PROBLEM AND WANTS TO FIX IT

In this scenario, the customer recognizes that he or she has a problem and wants to solve it. Here, the exchange between Bev and Joe might look like this.

Bev: Thanks for coming, Joe. We need to change ad agencies because we are just not happy with the sales results our ad campaigns are generating. We also aren't satisfied with the image that we are projecting to the marketplace. So, we thought we would explore some alternatives to our current ad agency. That's where you come in. How do you think you could help us?

Joe: I hope we can. But I'm going to need to ask you several questions to find out just how we might be able to offer the best solutions to your sales performance and image issues. Is that OK?

Bev: Of course. Fire away.

Joe: You said your ad campaigns were unsatisfactory when it came to sales results. Why do you think this was the case? This will help us not to make the same mistake.

Bev: Well, our biggest problem in that area was that we didn't appeal to the right market segment, i.e., the 21- to 35-year-olds.

Joe: I see. So you basically want us to put together a mock ad campaign on how we would go about capturing that business, is that right?

Bev: Basically.

Joe: Okay, we will do that, but before we do, let me ask you a few more questions about the characteristics of the people within that age group that you wish to target, if you don't mind?

Bev: Go right ahead, Joe.

Joe: Well, my first question focuses on what the characteristics are of the people who are currently buying.

What advances the sale is showing buyers the solutions to their problems when their pain is great enough to warrant a change or getting them to see their problems as big enough to solve with solutions that only you can provide. If you can't do that, you may do a lot of talking, but you won't get very far toward sustaining a business relationship.

FINDING OUT IF THE BUYER WANTS TO SOLVE THE PROBLEM

As we've seen, it's much easier to get customers to buy your solution when the problem is one that they themselves want to solve. To figure out whether the buyer wants to solve the problem, salespeople should consider the following questions: Does the customer view the problem as big enough to solve? And what does the customer see as the value of solving this problem?

DOES THE CUSTOMER VIEW THE PROBLEM AS BIG ENOUGH TO SOLVE? Here are examples of questions you could ask:

△ Is this an issue that you feel you need to address?

△ It sounds like that is a pretty sizable problem. Would you like to explore some possible solutions, or is it perhaps not serious enough to solve just yet?

WHAT DOES THE CUSTOMER SEE AS THE VALUE OF SOLVING THIS PROBLEM? Here are some sample questions:

△ How would it help you if you were able to fix this problem?

△ What do you see as the benefits of addressing this issue?

△ Are there any other benefits or value to you in solving the problem?

△ Do you see other ways in which solving this problem might help you?

DON'T OFFER SOLUTIONS TO EVERY CUSTOMER PROBLEM

It's important to wait until the customer perceives the problem as serious enough to solve. Psychologically, a solution has less impact on the customer when he or she is not ready to solve the problem than when he or she is ready to solve it. Therefore, top performers, since they are putting the customer first, will invariably withhold their solutions until they feel that these solutions will have the greatest customer impact—that is, until the customer perceives the problem as sizable enough to solve. Unless the customer tells the salesperson that he or she wants to solve the problem, the only way the salesperson is going to know for sure whether the customer sees the problem as sizable enough to solve is to ask the customer. Jim Preston, former president of Norwood Industries, located in Austin, Texas, said it best: "If a salesperson wants to aggravate someone, just let them try to solve a problem that the customer isn't ready to solve yet."

When you identify and try to develop the client's needs, you're in a better position to know whether the client sees the problem as big enough to warrant buying the service or product being offered. While prospects may admit that a problem exists, if they don't think the problem is serious enough—especially if there's a lot of risk associated with the solution—they won't buy. Once again, people are most receptive to solutions when the pain of making a change is less than the pain of staying the same.

Why would you ever want to offer a solution unless you were certain (either because you were told by the customer or because you asked the customer) that the customer was ready for one? Well, the answer is simple: You wouldn't. Prescribing surgery (the solution) without proper diagnosis (the probing/investigating) is malpractice (*not a good thing*).

ACTION POINTS

→ *Leave some issues on the table.* Don't try to solve all the customer's problems. Don't try to answer every objection. The more reasons you give to support your argument, the weaker your argument becomes.[13]

→ *Show courtesy and respect.* Always display concern for the customer's problems and respect for the customer's perception of these problems.

→ *Listen, test understanding, and clarify what the speaker says.* Occasionally ask the speaker if this is what he or she means. As Neil Rackham points out, use the customer's actual words, not a paraphrase. That way you can more easily come back to clarify or explore points. For example, "You said that your existing equipment suffers from, as you put it, 'fundamental design inefficiency.' Could you say more about that?"

→ *Separate problems to be solved and problems to be left alone.* Separate customer problems into two categories: those that the customer wants to solve and those that the customer is willing to live with.

→ *Don't offer unwelcome solutions.* Offer solutions only to those problems that the client is interested in solving.

SALES TRUTH 3: Offer solutions to problems the prospect *wants* to solve.

PRINCIPLE

get the most out of your best people

A TOP sales organization is able to get the most out of the best people. This starts with recruiting and hiring the best. Top sales organizations have highly effective processes for attracting and recruiting top-notch sales reps. Not only do these companies interview at top business schools, but they also actively participate in business school and other campus functions in order to get their name and reputation in front of the best students. They network within their own organizations to find the best new recruits and never lose sight of the need to develop their employees. They realize that top-notch selling isn't a natural talent. Successful companies use all available resources to improve the skills of their sales team—including academic classes. As one might expect, the interview process (both internal and external) in these organizations is grueling.

For example, Andersen Consulting actively participates in information sessions that offer it the opportunity to explain the career opportunities within the organization to groups of students at the Kelley School of Business at Indiana University. These sessions help students learn not only what it takes to be successful in the business world, but also what it takes to be successful at that particular company. Besides Andersen Consulting, the 200-plus companies that participate include Procter & Gamble, Motorola, ExxonMobil, Ernst & Young, Bank of America, E & J Gallo, Johnson & Johnson, 3M, PricewaterhouseCoopers, Eli Lilly, and CDW, to name just a few.[1] Some of these companies select recruiters with personal ties to Indiana University (or whatever university they are recruiting at) in the hope that these recruiters will relate better to students, thus enhancing the company's chances of attracting the best candidates.

One way in which some top sales companies recruit top-notch candidates for sales positions is through Baylor University's Center for Professional Selling. Under the direction of Terry Loe, Ph.D., Baylor's Center for Professional Selling conducts an "Academic World Series" of Professional Selling that is open to qualifying students from colleges and universities around the country. In role-plays, the students who qualify get to conduct "real life" sales interviews with "professional buyers." These role-plays help the participating students to develop their selling skills. Recruiters from well-known companies like EDS, Wilsonart International, and Xerox observe these sales role-plays. This puts them in a position to preview the "sales stars" of the future and get a head start on their recruiting efforts.[2]

DEVELOPING PEOPLE

Recruitment is one way in which companies can get the best people. Top sales companies also network within their own organizations to find the best people, as well as never losing sight of the need to develop their own salespeople. One *Fortune* 50 corporation took the development of its people to a higher level when it transferred a manager with ten years' experience in its service organization to the sales division to conduct the training of new hires. The premise for this type of cross-divisional or cross-department training is that the more business perspectives people have, the better they will be able to serve the customer.[3]

There are several sales traps that, if not avoided, can cause talented recruits to be less than successful once they begin to sell professionally. For example, some recruits believe that they are a failure if customers reject them or believe that academic classes don't help in the real world. They believe that the evidence supports the theory that you either have it or you don't. However, these three mistaken beliefs are traps not only for the salesperson, but also for the company that stubbornly believes that stars are born, not made.

*   *   *

sales trap 4:
Rejection Is Failure

When I was manager of training and development at the Xerox International Training Center, I was asked to work with Ellen, a new sales rep who had a territory in the rural area of a Midwestern state. Unfortunately, she was struggling to achieve her sales quota. Here's what happened:

> Ellen wanted to become a top sales performer. This was not surprising, since she had always excelled in sports, school activities, and academics. During one of my visits, her manager asked if I would meet with her, tag along on her field sales calls, and give her any necessary feedback and advice.
>
> The next day I traveled with her on her sales calls. I sat back, observed, and kept my mouth shut. Ellen was charming, charismatic, and dynamic. She appeared to be an excellent hire. She was strong on interpersonal skills. All her customers and prospects liked her. After the fourth sales call, however, I began to see an emerging pattern of sales-skill inefficiency. Ellen shied away from asking customers about their problems, difficulties, or dissatisfactions.
>
> Later, I suggested to her that she begin to ask more problem-focused questions, questions directed at discovering problems, difficulties, or dissatisfactions. She said that she didn't mind gathering situational and background information from the customers, but she was hesitant about delving into their problems. Since the company training program at the time was based upon a probing model, it was easy to give her specific suggestions for improvement.

At first, she was excited about trying something new and "simple." But, of course, nothing is as simple as it first appears to be. In applying the probing model, Ellen quickly became discouraged. Her performance got worse instead of better. Customers were becoming annoyed with her. Some even asked her to leave the office. Ellen couldn't stand the rejection. She hated those problem questions. "They only annoy my customers," she complained.

This charming and likable person seemed to be losing her interpersonal skills. And then there was the problem of her deteriorating performance. "My customers think I'm prying too much," she said. "I'm a failure."

Ellen, an outstanding hire, was about to give up because she thought she was about to fail.

GIVING UP IS FAILURE

Fortunately, Ellen didn't fail. As you'll see, we found a way to get the most out of her, to redirect her so that she could succeed for herself and for the company.

Rejection is not failure. The only way people fail in sales is by giving up. In the videotape *Do Right*, former Notre Dame football coach Lou Holtz says that we all face adversity in life, some of us more than others. According to Holtz, the people who win are the people who handle adversity best. They're the ones who don't give up.

As it turned out, Ellen ended up handling her adversity like a winner. She didn't give up. She identified one specific area of weakness in her skill of asking focused questions. Before her sales calls, she and I "wordsmithed" examples of problem questions that she expected to ask in upcoming sales interviews. She began anew and worked hard to effect a behavioral change in her selling. This story has a wonderful ending. Her vibrant personality, coupled with her increasingly effective probing skills, enabled her to become the top salesperson in her division in the central United States for Xerox.

The trait of never giving up and always coming back to fight another round is lodged deeply in the outlook of successful people and is a trait that recruiters cherish in a candidate. As former Xerox recruiter John Cuny stated, "Show me someone who won't give up at the first sign of adversity and I'll show you a person who will be a winner someday."

REJECTION

It's pretty easy to believe that rejection means failure. It's human nature to feel bad about rejection, to take it personally. But this just isn't true in sales. In sales, although "yes" means success, "no" *doesn't* necessarily mean failure. When customers say "no," they're just saying that they don't want to buy right now. And that's okay. They're *not* saying that the salesperson is a failure. Salespeople who believe this fallacy aren't looking at the big picture. They don't see that a "no" is just a rock to be hurdled on the uphill road to top sales performance. They see rejection as failure and see themselves as victims. Managers who let salespeople believe this won't get the most from the best.

SALES CALL RELUCTANCE

The consequences of falling into this sales trap are serious. If you believe that rejection is failure, the chances are good that pretty soon you won't want to make sales calls. You'll want to sit on the bench. Sales call reluctance—the fear of making sales calls—may come when a salesperson:

△ Feels inadequately prepared or trained to make the call

△ Lacks the drive and motivation to make the call

△ Believes that, because of his or her workload, he or she doesn't have enough time to make new business sales calls

△ Doesn't like the job and so doesn't make the effort

△ Doesn't believe that new business calls are as crucial to his or her success as retaining current customers

△ Fears rejection by the customer on the call

Although several of these reasons may keep a salesperson from making sales calls, in my experience it's the last one—fear of the buyer's rejection—that's at the top of most people's list. Ask yourself this question: Are you generally more excited about visiting someone who *wants to see you* or someone who *may or may not want to see you?*

The belief that rejection is failure is simply the wrong inference to make from the facts. In sales, everyone faces rejection every day, and no one likes it—not even top performers.

SUCCESSFUL FAILURE

Top performers don't give up. They've embraced the concept of successful failure. Successful failure is learning from your mistakes so that you don't make the same mistake again. Thomas Edison experienced 10,000 failures before he hit on success and invented the light bulb. Edison counted all these failures as part of his success and said, "Our greatest weakness lies in giving up. The most certain way to succeed is to always try just one more time."

Successful failure incorporates the idea that if you accept failure and learn from it, you're more likely to be successful in the future. Babe Ruth had 714 home runs—but also 1,330 strikeouts. Hank Aaron, who beat Babe Ruth's record, had 755 home runs and 1,383 strikeouts. Mickey Mantle had 536 home runs and 1,710 strikeouts. It's pretty easy to see the similarity between the home runs (making the sale) and the strikeouts (making the call).

LEARNING FROM MISTAKES

Successful failure consists of two components:

1. *Double-loop learning.* Top performers use a learning technique called "double-loop" learning.[4] They stand back from the failure and mentally review the situation. They analyze what they thought they were doing versus what they actually did, ask for and accept feedback, and then practice and redefine what they want to do the next time. *They learn by relearning.* In particular, top performers often ask others for help, input, and feedback about why they failed. Double-loop learning helps you improve by teaching you not to repeat mistakes.

   Top performers spend considerable time reviewing and debriefing their sales calls in order not to repeat their mistakes. However, the time the consultant spends in reviewing and debriefing calls isn't the deciding factor between success and failure. The deciding factor tends to be the quality of feedback from the manager, coupled with the consultant's desire not to make the same error again.[5]

2. *Not giving up.* There is no substitute for field sales experience. You can't learn how to sell by watching videos of inspirational sales leaders. How does a salesperson get experience and at the same time increase his or her chances for success? The answer is simple in theory, but hard in practice: You must simply get out and make the sales calls. You have to be up at bat.

KNOWING YOUR NUMBERS

When salespeople "get over it" and adopt the more positive philosophy that not all sales calls will be successful, they need to have a number in mind, a success percentage of calls that result in specific, agreed-upon actions between salesperson and client that they will need to achieve in order to meet or exceed their quotas. For example, what percentage of your sales calls do you target to result in an action step such as a proposal, a demonstration, an introduction of your boss, a study, and so forth?

Many *Fortune* 500 companies set activity targets for their salespeople. They expect their salespeople to make x number of sales calls per day or per week, to deliver y number of proposals, and so forth. These targets result from the belief that the more sales calls that someone makes, the more likely it is that a customer will "stick an order" in the salesperson's pocket. This is probably true for transactional sales, but it isn't true for the consultative type of sales.

Only masochists *like* rejection. But top consultants recognize that it comes with the territory and that not everyone needs their products or services. They may even recommend someone who has better solutions.

ACTION POINTS

→ *Keep learning and improving.* Top salespeople never stop learning. And they pay special attention when things go wrong. The best learning experiences come from successful failure.

→ *Set sales activity standards for the transactional sale.* With transactional sales, results are about making a lot of sales calls, i.e., quantity. In other words, work hard.

→ *Develop sales strategies for the consultative sale.* Unlike the transactional or small sale, where sales activities drive performance results, in the more complex consultative sale, the driving factor tends to be the development and execution of the correct sales strategies—i.e., quality before quantity. For example, if the customer is in the evaluation of options phase of the decision process, your strategy might be to identify how the customer ranks the decision criteria on a scale from crucial to incidental. Probing effectively for this ranking would be the way to execute this strategy.

SALES TRUTH 4: Giving up is failure.

----

sales trap 5:
Academic Studies Aren't Helpful in Real-World Sales

Here's the mistaken belief: Academic studies aren't helpful in the real world of sales. ("Academic studies" here refers to both formal college sales classes and academically validated research.) Practitioners will often say, "What do academics know about selling? Many of them haven't ever sold."

But this prejudice is wrong and usually comes from lack of familiarity with what's going on in academic institutions today and with the published sales research. Academic studies (with some caveats) can help in getting the most out of the best.

THE DIFFICULTY OF STUDYING SALES

Over lunch one day, Jim, a first-line sales manager who was recruiting at the Kelley School of Business, asked me, "Do you believe that college sales courses help students sell better once we hire them? And," he went on, "do you think that the students who do best in your sales classes will be the ones who will do the best in the field?"

Since I was a teacher, it was hard for me not to just say, "Yes, of course," to both of Jim's questions. But I didn't.

The Institute for Global Sales Studies at Indiana University, where I work, had not set up any metrics or research methodology to effectively measure the impact of college sales courses on real-life sales. Nor did I know of any other academic institution that had researched this.

Even if we wanted to measure the success of students who did take college sales classes against the success of those who didn't, there would be worrisome questions. First of all, how would we define "success?" Do we define it in terms of sales revenues, and if so, how do we factor in the different prices of products and services across different industries? And once we defined success in sales, it wouldn't be easy to draw a direct cause-and-effect relationship between sales classes in college and sales performance in the business world. How would we take into account such factors as raw talent and the issue of recruiting top people who are right off the bat more likely to succeed than others? How would we factor in questions relating to the student's industry, the student's territory, and the success of the product being sold relative to the marketplace competition? And what about the student's knowledge of the product, attitude, passion for the job, manager, on-the-job training, competition from other sales reps on staff, and so forth? These troublesome questions could have a serious impact on the "truth."

DO SALES COURSES HELP?

Formal studies at the college level do help in sales. It is just difficult to know whether they help a little or a lot. Such studies may or may not be high on the list of attributes that help a student succeed—attributes such as a methodical thought process, creative thinking, capacity to listen, degree of curiosity, and the desire to understand and make a contribution. These other attributes may be more important than studying sales formally in college.

REDUCED RISK IN HIRING STUDENTS WHO STUDIED SALES

College recruits who have studied sales may be less risky as new hires because they have *chosen* sales. They are more likely to be well suited to sales as a career and to stay in it long enough for their employers to see the return on the company's investment in training them. R. R. Donnelley & Sons, for example, is narrowing its salesperson recruiting effort to schools that offer sales courses. This way, the company can be more certain that it hires people who actually want to sell.[6]

Bridget Momcilovich, a senior manager with the Xerox Corporation, agrees. "Students who have taken sales courses at a college level may not be more equipped to do the job better here at Xerox than students who have not taken sales classes, but at least they have a better idea of what they are getting themselves into. In my opinion, this helps us reduce our hiring risks."

SALES COURSES AS A SCREENING METHOD

According to Dr. Frank Acito, chairman of the marketing department at Indiana University, "A high percentage—more than 50 percent—of our marketing graduates end up taking a sales position of one type or another. Sales courses are helpful to them in the sense that they give the students an opportunity to more fully understand what they will be expected to do once they start their job."

Another reason that it is helpful to hire graduates who have degrees in sales is that they have often learned what not to do based upon the latest research. One former student at Indiana University hadn't intended to go into sales. Even though she had the aptitude for sales, Kristin Johnson, like many students, was reluctant to pursue a sales career because she thought it would require her to be "aggressive" toward other people in order to succeed. Fortunately, the classes at Indiana University are structured around the latest research, which shows that in today's modern sales world, a person doesn't have to be aggressive in order to succeed. (See also Sales Trap 1, "You Must Be Aggressive to Succeed in Sales.")

After graduating, Kristin took a sales position with a market-dominant news media company and performed well. She is now working for an international pharmaceutical corporation, a blue-chip company that is very selective in its hiring.

Kristin believes the sales classes helped her tremendously in her sales career, and we can probably conclude that Kristin would not have taken a sales position if she had not taken her two sales classes. According to Kristin, "Those sales classes were instrumental in helping me select a career and valuable in helping me do well once on the job." Certainly in this sense sales classes help screen for those who have an aptitude and are interested in sales as a career, factors that are likely to help lead to greater efficiency on the job.

SALES RESEARCH

Published sales research is also controversial. Many people routinely dismiss validated sales research by saying that it's not useful to practitioners. What have sales researchers who use academic methods or validated research been able to contribute to the sales field or to sales courses?

One eminent sales researcher who made it to the top of the sales profession is Neil Rackham, who observed 35,000 sales calls in 23 countries over 12 years, looking for what made salespeople successful. Rackham performed his postgraduate work in behavioral psychology at the University of Sheffield in England. He is an example of a research academician whose strategies have greatly benefited the sales profession. Companies such as AT&T, IBM, Xerox, Microsoft, and UPS have used his research findings to help them mold their own field sales forces into a formidable marketing tool.[7]

Dr. Rosann Spiro, former chairperson of the American Marketing Association and currently a full professor at the Kelley School of Business at Indiana University, has conducted studies that show that salespeople who are more adaptive to different types of people tend to be more successful. Dr. Barton Weitz, professor of marketing at the University of Florida, has performed similar research in the field of adaptive selling and the role it plays in successful sales call outcomes.[8] There are several programs that use this method, including Wilson Learning, Inc., and DISC.

There are different research methodologies used by today's leading researchers. Each method has advantages and disadvantages. Three popular methods follow.

BEHAVIOR-BASED. Behavior-based researchers observe the verbal behaviors used by the salesperson and track the outcome of the sales call. This method is expensive and takes a long time, but it is probably the most accurate.

CUSTOMER-BASED. This method involves interviewing customers to identify what characteristics they prefer in salespeople. It is a relatively quick way to gather information. Unfortunately, customers talk in generalities, such as, "I want a salesperson who is concerned about me" or "Follow-up is important."

EXPERT-BASED. This method involves interviewing top-performing salespeople and asking them why they have been successful. It appears to have the most credibility and is also relatively fast. Unfortunately, what appears to be its strength is really its drawback: Top performers don't always know what makes them successful, and their opinions may run contrary to scientific research findings. For example, for over fifty years—from 1925 to 1980—successful trainers and salespeople believed that open-ended questions led to sales call success more than closed-ended questions. This belief was refuted by original research undertaken by Neil Rackham in the 1970s.[9]

COLLEGES AND UNIVERSITIES OFFERING COURSES IN SALES

Historically, sales has been treated as a second-class citizen at academic institutions. But that's beginning to change. More and more leading academic institutions are offering undergraduate sales courses, and companies are seeing the benefit of hiring graduates who have studied sales.[10] The University of Akron is one of the very few institutions offering a major in sales.[11] The following list shows some of the institutions that offer sales courses:

Partial List of Colleges and Universities Offering Sales Courses[12]

Ball State University

Baylor University

Brigham Young University

Butler University

California State University, Sacramento

Central Michigan University

College of St. Catherine

Colorado State University

Cornell

Curtin University of Technology

Florida Gulf Coast University

Indiana University

Illinois State University

Mankato State University

Northern Illinois University

Ohio University

Purdue University

St. Cloud State University

Texas A & M University

Tuskegee University

University of Akron

University of Alabama at Birmingham

University of Central Florida

University of Cincinnati

University of Florida

University of Georgia

University of Kentucky

University of North Carolina at Wilmington

University of South Florida

University of Tennessee

University of Toledo

HIRING SALES STUDENTS

To get the most out of the best, companies are hiring more sales students. There are many people who back into sales as a career, and these people need on-the-job training and skill building. Companies like Minnesota Mining and Manufacturing Co. (3M) want to increase the number of new salespeople who are already trained by hiring graduates who have studied sales. In fact, 3M is handing out hundreds of thousands of dollars to schools that are willing to teach sales skills. The College of St. Catherine in Minnesota and Tuskegee University in Alabama are both adding sales courses with money from 3M.[13] Approximately 80 percent of the Kelley School of Business's marketing graduates take at least one sales or sales management class before they graduate. The University of Akron in Ohio reports that from 1996 to 1999, every one of its sales students was offered a job after graduation.[14]

ACTION POINTS

→ *Seek to hire students who have taken undergraduate sales courses.* They know what they are getting themselves into, which may help reduce their failure rate. Investigate the courses a student has taken. Find out what the course methodology was and whether the statements and findings documented in the books used are based upon a particular research methodology or upon just one expert opinion (which may or may not be right).

→ *Use the research-based methods of the leading sales researchers.* There's too much opinion and not enough research in sales. Take advantage of the work done by leading sales researchers to improve sales effectiveness.

SALES TRUTH 5: **Academic studies may reduce hiring risk, and academic research provides validated techniques.**

---

sales trap 6:
Either Salespeople Have It or They Don't

Are salespeople born or made?

Many people believe that they're born.

But that's a fallacy, and if you want to get the most out of the best, don't fall into Sales Trap 6. Salespeople are developed, and it takes them time to develop.

"It's easy to believe that salespeople either have it or they don't," says Dr. Rosann Spiro, former chairperson of the American Marketing Association. "But the research shows that salespeople improve with practice and experience, with average performers improving the most."[15]

Sales Trap 6 is common. "It's in the DNA," some claim, "so why bother trying to improve?" However, most people who develop into top performers do so over time, rather than immediately. The suggestion that these people develop into top performers because "they had it from the get-go" and that they are just "fulfilling their destiny" is a fallacy that fails to recognize that top performers needed to develop along the way.

WHAT SALESPEOPLE DO TO IMPROVE

The Dartmouth Group has observed thousands of successful salespeople and many top performers. The common denominator among all of them was that they improved over time because they did one or more of the following:

1. Analyzed what went right or wrong on a sales call

2. Participated in company sales training programs that provided reinforcement and feedback from front-line sales managers

3. Received frequent constructive feedback from their bosses

4. Reviewed taped sales calls for errors and missed opportunities

5. Took part in and reviewed simulated and videotaped role-play sales situations with a manager, mentor, or colleague

Top salespeople are good at "thought process" and "thought link" development, the ability to link one issue to another in a sales call or other customer conversation. Salespeople need to be able to think. Thinking enables them to better understand customers' problems and to link these problems to still other problems the customers may have in their companies.

Salespeople require development—some more than others. Regardless of how they develop, it's clear that few of the top salespeople would have achieved success without training and development. Jon King, former senior manager with Xerox and later chief marketing officer for Ikon Office Solutions, put it this way: "If the majority of people believe that a person is born to succeed, then why don't they go find them and stop investing their money in training? It's just not that simple. Some people may have more raw talent, but what they do with that talent is another issue."

DEBUNKING THE "SUPERSTAR" THEORY

One reason people defend the "either you have it or you don't" idea is the "superstar" discovery. Occasionally, a recruiter or manager will "discover" a person who seems to have all the attributes of a successful salesperson. He or she is engaging, has strong interpersonal skills, is disciplined, has excellent grades, and always seems to succeed, and the recruiter basically tells the interviewer that "what you see is what you get." Admittedly, what one sees is impressive.

Why doesn't the occasional superstar prove that "either you have it or you don't"? There are two factors that need to be considered: (1) The individual may have had more development opportunities along the way than others had, and (2) the individual may not have the drive to be successful once he or she is on the job. For example, I recall very vividly a "superstar" that the management staff in the local district office at Xerox believed would be sensational. I too strongly believed in this person and his credentials.

Throughout the ninety-day training program, he led his new hire training class. One manager even suggested that this star could become the heir apparent to our CEO someday. All the sales managers wanted him on their sales team. He did turn out to be successful, but he was not considered a top performer after five years. Why did he fail to be a top performer when he had all the apparent attributes of a superstar?

Who knows for sure? Maybe, in the end, he didn't like the job well enough. There might have been too much inside and outside pressure on him to succeed. Perhaps Xerox sales management was to blame for not making him more accountable because they didn't feel that he needed to be monitored, inspected, and reviewed as rigorously as his peers. In the end, Joe Cegala, who headed up the service operation in the central United States for NCR a few years back, probably summed it up the best with his favorite motto, "Potential is interesting, but performance is everything."

PERSONALITY TYPE

People incorrectly attribute sales success to personality. That's the second reason for "either you have it or you don't." For example, let's say that an individual with a dynamic and charming personality is a top performer. It is easy to conclude that the person is a top performer *because* of his personality and interpersonal skills. (This may be partially true. Interpersonal verbal skills may give that person an edge when it comes to applying sales skills.)

What may not be taken into account, however, is that this likable person may also sell more effectively. For example, he or she may probe for the customer's needs more effectively than an average performer. Our hypothetical salesperson with the dynamic and charming personality may also create more value in his or her solutions than an average performer. How do you account for a person who doesn't have a sparkling personality but is nevertheless a top performer? As Susan Woods, a former training manager for a regional bank and now with The Dartmouth Group, Ltd., observed, "Why are there people with strong interpersonal skills that seem to remain in a 'state of mediocrity' while other people with average interpersonal skills become top performers?"

If you want to get the most out of the best, develop your people. They need it (some more than others). Salespeople are made, not born.

ACTION POINTS

→ *Be patient.* The Dartmouth Group, Ltd., estimates that it takes nine to eighteen months of dedicated effort to master probing skills (asking good business questions that focus on problems and the value of solutions) and to become unconsciously competent in their use.[16] As Neil Rackham says of the SPIN® method, "If it were easy, everybody would be doing it. It's hard—that's why the few people who do it well are so very successful."[17]

→ *Give constructive feedback.* Constructive feedback tells salespeople what they are doing wrong and shows them specifically how to correct it. Without feedback, sales performance and sales results suffer for both the individual and his or her company.

→ *Give consistent feedback that doesn't exclude anyone.* There is a tendency to not provide feedback to your top performers and your "heir apparent," but this is a mistake. Top performers like solid, constructive feedback, too. That may be why they became top performers to begin with. Even Michael Jordan sought and received constructive feedback from his coach at North Carolina, Dean Smith, and from his coach with the Chicago Bulls, Phil Jackson.

→ *Remember that salespeople are made, not born.* It takes time for salespeople to get better and to develop. The only way to fail to develop is to give up (see Sales Trap 4, "Rejection Is Failure"). Giving up on your personal development may be the only thing worse than failure because it means that you are giving up on yourself, your hopes and dreams. In the movie *Flashdance*, Nick (Michael Nouri) says to Alex (Jennifer Beals), "Alex, without hopes and dreams, we die."

SALES TRUTH 6: Salespeople are *developed*, not *born*.

PRINCIPLE 3

train
effectively

LEADING sales companies, such as IBM, Merck, and Motorola, have highly effective sales training programs. Not only do they select programs based on effective methodologies and not just on top performer opinions (see Sales Trap 5, "Academic Studies Aren't Helpful in Real-World Sales"), but they also use these programs to increase the sales team's efficiency in a variety of other ways.

COMMON LANGUAGE

One key function of a sales training program is to provide salespeople, sales managers, and consultants with a common language to reinforce the strategies, tactics, and behaviors taught in the training modules (see Sales Trap 7). Top sales companies use sales training programs to develop a *lingua franca*, or common language, about sales. Thus, companies need to be cautioned against throwing in the proverbial kitchen sink. If they try to cover everything under the sun, the deluge of new words thrown at the salespeople in a "data dump" will confuse them. The lingua franca facilitates sales coordination, customer service efficiency, and employee transfers. People can transfer from department to department or division to division within the company more efficiently, because they don't have to learn an entirely new language and culture. This common language also helps salespeople from different departments to plan and implement cross-selling opportunities more effectively.

Perhaps one of the best examples is the banking industry. Many banks have retail people (branch banking personnel who work with consumers) who are involved in smaller transactional selling (checking accounts, savings accounts, credit card services, credit lines, ATM cards, etc.). Yet they also have commercial lending officers who are involved in consultative selling (premium business loans and cash management services) to medium and large businesses. The sales models used on the branch side (to sell small, simple products and services) are different from those on the commercial banking side (to sell large, complex products and services). In order to accommodate this difference, banks with strong selling cultures use sales training programs in which the same language is adapted for both uses. With the same sales language, people from the branch banking side can more easily communicate with people on the commercial banking side. As Gerald Rush, senior vice president of Bank One, says, "It is easier for us to cross-sell our services to our customers, thus solving more of their problems and creating delivered value to them, when our people talk the same language."

CUSTOMIZING

The training programs chosen by top sales organizations incorporate the organization's value and belief system. The courses are, in a sense, *customized* around the corporate business culture. This shared value system helps to ensure that everyone in the sales organization has the same values, such as "focus on the customer first" or "maintain strong ethical standards." For example, the customization of a company's training program might include an emphasis on questioning to display concern toward the customer rather than an emphasis on aggressive closing techniques that could aggravate the customer and make him or her feel unimportant. If a shared value is to put customers first, then the training program and the customization of it should reflect this value, not counteract it (see Sales Trap 7).

Top-flight sales organizations will often customize sales training for specialized markets. They do this by outsourcing research projects to a sales training and consulting research firm. Research firms conduct field observations in order to tailor-make sales training for specific markets. Eli Lilly followed such a procedure, as was explained to me by its manager of training and development.[1] To put it another way, the customizing of the content is important, since adults learn better when they can relate and apply concepts, models, and strategies to their actual work.

A final thought about customizing: In general, the more customized the sales training program is to the participant's day-to-day job, the more effective the program will be.[2] The more strategically customized a sales skill training program can be, the better it will be understood and applied by participants. But even if the program is highly customized, it will not be effective long if it is not reinforced by feedback from the manager.

*   *   *

sales trap 7:
It's the Content of the Skill Training That Matters Most

Managers spend hours sweating over all the sales skill training courses available today. There's nothing wrong with that, unless they expect the payoff from sales training to come solely from the *content* of the training course, believing the fallacy that the content of the course is the most important part of training.

It isn't.

If you want to get a performance edge from sales training, you have to provide feedback and reinforcement after the course. Otherwise, the training won't be effective.

FOUR BASIC TYPES OF COURSES

Having said that, it's helpful to review the four basic types of sales courses that are available on the market today. An informed consumer of sales training has to at least be familiar with these four categories. Each category has a perspective that seems to have the potential to make a contribution to an individual's sales skill development. As you might expect, the quality of the program content, architecture, and exercises vary from program to program.

ATTITUDINAL METHOD. Probably the most popular and widely used approach to skill development in this category is Professional Selling Skills, better known as PSS. The PSS approach was developed by the Xerox Corporation, distributed by its Xerox Learning Systems division, and used by IBM, American Airlines, and Prudential, among others. Xerox used PSS until the early 1980s. Since so many companies used the PSS approach, it was often referred to as "the Xerox course."[3]

PSS focuses on the customer's attitude, and thus it's known as a course that uses the attitudinal approach. The attitudinal approach suggests that a customer will have one of four attitudes: acceptance, indifference, rejection, or skepticism. The seller must select the appropriate communication model(s) that correspond(s) to the particular attitude that the buyer displays.

There are six communication models (the names have changed since PSS was created):

△ Probing

△ Supporting

△ Objection handling

△ Proof

△ Closing

△ Benefit statement

For example, if a customer's attitude is one of acceptance, a salesperson may want to use the support model, in which she or he agrees with the customer's positive comments, or the salesperson might decide to use the closing model. This approach develops a salesperson's conversational effectiveness by helping the salesperson to adapt readily to the buyer's attitude.

ADAPTIVE OR SOCIAL-STYLE APPROACH. The second category is referred to as the adaptive or social-style approach. This method suggests that there are four basic social styles that people can have. While the names for the four styles may vary, the intent of the program offerings in this category is to recognize that people with each of the four social styles process information differently. Therefore, the logical conclusion of this approach is that top-performing salespeople should not only adapt to a buyer's particular social style but also communicate to that person the way that person likes to be

communicated to. For example, one set of social-style labels might
be Driver, Expressive, Amiable, and Analytic. Let's say a buyer is an
Analytic. The social-style approach suggests that the sales consultant communicate with the Analytic in detail and present thorough
and footnoted proposals. If the buyer happens to be a Driver, the
consultant would be advised to avoid detail and provide executive
summaries. The point is that this category of sales skill approach
highlights the idea that people differ and that you need to adapt
your style of communication based on the particular social type you
are interacting with. Programs in this category attempt to achieve
three basic objectives:

1. Be able to recognize each of the social style types

2. Be able to identify each of the types

3. Be able to adapt your communication style based upon
   social type

Again, the content, architecture, and exercises will differ among
different programs, but the essence of this category remains the
same: People are different; therefore, treat them the way they want
to be treated, not the way you want to be treated.

Perhaps the single drawback to this approach lies in the difficulty of correctly assessing an individual's social style.[4] For example, an Analytic who might usually be considered a low reactor
type might be perceived as a Driver when under pressure by his or
her boss to perform. The adaptive or social-style approach is an
interesting approach that is usually received well by salespeople.[5]
Jim Cotterill, president of jcotterill.com, demonstrated the Driver
social style when he said, "Consultants visit with me and believe
they should spend considerable time developing a high trust relationship with me. I want to say to them, 'I've got enough friends

and acquaintances; I don't need any more. What I need is someone who can solve my key business problems.'"

LEARNING-STYLE APPROACH. This category suggests that each person will learn in one of three ways: visually, auditorily, or kinesthetically. For example, if the buyer is primarily a visual learner, a sales consultant might want to appeal to this person's learning style by using graphs, charts, and pictures in the presentation. If a person is an auditory learner, then the consultant might want to focus his or her efforts on articulating solutions or implementation processes effectively. And if an individual learns better kinesthetically—by touch and feel—then the consultant might invite the person to participate in the demonstration of the product or service.

As with the social-style category, it's hard for the sales consultant to accurately identify the particular learning style a buyer predominantly uses. Continued observations regarding eye and body movements are necessary to help pinpoint a person's particular style.

NEEDS-BASED APPROACH. Needs-based programs are arguably the most popular type of training program. This approach basically suggests that customers have two types of needs: those associated with a problem they are willing to live with and those associated with a problem they want to solve. A customer is more likely to be receptive to a sales solution when he or she perceives a problem that is serious enough for him or her to solve. (See also Sales Trap 3, "It's Best to Offer Solutions to Problems You See.") A salesperson uncovers problems in the first category and develops them into the second category by asking particular types of questions.[6]

The drawback to this approach is that it's a big challenge to get salespeople to ask the right type of questions. (It isn't that difficult to identify which types of questions salespeople should ask; what's difficult is getting salespeople to ask them.) Asking the right kind of questions naturally and smoothly takes a lot of practice and feedback.

COACHING AND FEEDBACK

Here's the rub: No matter what course salespeople take, it won't help them sell better unless the sales skills are reinforced afterward. The idea that sales skill training works without reinforcement is a fallacy. In 1979, a study at Xerox revealed that thirty days after sales-skill-based training, the participants had lost 87 percent of the behaviors that they had learned unless those behaviors were reinforced.[7] That means for each $1 that Xerox invested in sales skill training, it received only 13 cents back. In other words, coaching and feedback is worth about 87 cents on each dollar spent. With a return like this, why would anyone emphasize the content of the courses over coaching and reinforcement?

More than the content of courses, it's coaching, feedback, reinforcement, and implementation that are the keys to behavior changes that increase sales effectiveness. Managers from senior management all the way down to first-line management (with support from the sales training department) should see to it that coaching is taking place.

Karen Thor, executive vice president and CIO of National Commerce Bancorporation, put it succinctly: "We purchased the best content program in our opinion that money could buy, but it became clear that our training dollar investment totally hinged upon our ability to get our people to act differently on sales calls. In the end, coaching is 'where it's at.' No program is better than another without coaching. You coach an average program and you will get more out of it than if you have an outstanding program that is not coached at all."

ACTION POINTS

→ *Make sure coaching happens.* Develop a coaching process to achieve behavioral change. (See also Sales Trap 22, "Sales Managers Are Good Coaches"). Secure the commitment of managers from senior management to front-line management to coaching and reinforcement.

→ *Limit the number of people in coaching classes.* Don't overload the coach. Coaching more than three people at any point in time is not recommended for a first-line manager who already has a large span of control. Coaching and feedback tasks are time-consuming.

→ *Measure and monitor the results of coaching.* Take a baseline measurement of the behaviors of each participant as soon as possible after each training session. (This is usually done by the first-line manager.) Measure the behavioral change of each participant every thirty days.

→ *Recognize and reward behavioral changes.* Reinforce the coaching program by acknowledging new behaviors that salespeople exhibit. Award plaques. Create an atmosphere and culture that genuinely believes in improving sales performance through behavioral change and personal development.

SALES TRUTH 7: Sales skill training effectiveness is about coaching, not content.

---

sales trap 8:
Beginners Should Start With Comprehensive Training

More is better. That's the widespread belief when it comes to training beginners in sales. The assumption is that because beginners have so much to learn, they should get it all at once. During their initial sales training period, beginners are often given a comprehensive skill-based training program covering many strategies and tactics, so that they can pick and choose which ideas to implement. It's then assumed that they will be able to go out in the field and do what is expected. This is a fallacy.

I call this approach to training beginners "the Blitz," named after the blitz bombing of London by the Nazis in World War II. The Blitz approach blankets beginners with everything they could ever need to know about sales. It's total immersion. And it's devastating.

Why? Because comprehensive training overwhelms beginners. It's ineffective because beginners are not able to take in all the new material. For sales training effectiveness, introduce one skill at a time and reinforce it.

John Cuny, currently a consultant with Ernst & Young and former manager of training and development for Xerox, explains that he tries to keep his sales skill–based training simple. "The information included in our Buyer-Focused Selling program used at Document University in Leesburg, Virginia, is almost overwhelming. It's good content, but it is almost too much in too short a time. I tend to favor a 'less is more' approach rather than a 'more is better.' People can only learn so much at one time."[8]

Dr. Richard Ruff, president of Sales Momentum in Scottsdale, Arizona, said it this way: "Your best sports coaches recognize that they get behavioral change quicker from their players when they focus on one particular behavior at a time, whether it be blocking out in basketball, tackling in football, or tossing up the tennis ball in a serve. Most people, generally speaking, have difficulty trying to change several things at once. And, sales training programs that include so many behaviors and strategies to learn are less likely to work in the long run than programs that key in on just a few things for the consultant to change."

People are more motivated to learn when they are not deluged with things to think about. Knowledge isn't successfully transferred to behavior when it's hidden in a comprehensive training class. This is because behavioral change is harder than knowledge transfer. And behavioral change takes time. Sales training that focuses on one or two skills at a time provides ample opportunity for beginners to work more effectively in the field. Anything more than that overloads them. Perhaps Leon Edelsack, former senior vice president of Westinghouse's communication division, said it best: "I don't want our people to experience a data dump because it is like drinking water from a fire hose. It is too much and it doesn't satisfy anyone."

ACTION POINTS

For training organizations:

→ *Avoid the "data dump.* Take a "less is more" approach to sales skill training. New hires can't drink water from a fire hose.

→ *Change behavior one skill at a time.* To be effective, training should focus on one behavior at a time—for example, asking lots of questions versus giving lots of information.

For people who want to be top performers:

→ *Focus on one behavior to change at a time.* Practice. Get feedback from someone (your sales manager, your training manager, or a high-relationship customer) regarding how well you are doing with that particular behavior. Remember: Rome wasn't built in a day, and neither was the top performer.

SALES TRUTH 8: Adults learn best when they can relate strategies, tactics, skills, and information to what they do every day, so *train beginners with "less is more" in mind.*

PRINCIPLE

create
value

VALUE is defined as Benefits minus Cost (V = B – C). Cost doesn't just mean the price of the service, however. Today's customers look at total cost, both direct and indirect costs.

Direct costs are the dollar price plus other charges (installation for a piece of equipment, postinstallation service, etc.). Indirect costs include such things as career risk to the person or group of people making the decision, the hassle involved in changing, and corporate or other business risks associated with the change.

The price that today's customers will pay for a product or service must provide them with benefits equal to or greater than the dollars they pay. Most customers will not pay a higher price for a competing product unless they perceive that the value of that product outweighs the cost. Unfortunately, many customers do not perceive the added value that justifies the cost in many commodity products today.

Consultative salespeople are challenged to figure out a way to create value so that customers are willing to pay a little more for the products or services they offer. If they can't do this, they are forced to reduce their price in order to provide value.

Consultative selling of business services is especially interesting as a study in value creation, since these companies don't offer tangible products. Consulting firms such as McKinsey, for example, basically offer the intellectual property produced by their consultants. In order to solve customer problems, these consultants need to be able to think creatively, be self-confident, and have access to proprietary databases. The counsel and advice offered by leading sales, marketing, and consulting firms is almost solely focused on creating customer value—in other words, addressing customer needs and problems in depth. Sometimes salespeople believe they are creating value, only to discover later that the customer doesn't perceive the same value (see Sales Traps 10 and 11).

Of course, creating value for the customer is not always easy. As we mentioned under Principle 1, "Adopt an Outside Focus," creating customer value requires strong coordinating efforts between the sales and marketing departments. It's ultimately up to the first-line managers and the field salespeople to implement value creation.

BUSINESS ACUMEN AND KNOWLEDGE

Strong business acumen is also necessary if the salesperson is to create value. Salespeople who want to create value will need to view their clients from a holistic perspective. Top business schools promote this holistic approach by requiring an interdisciplinary rigor. Salespeople need to look at the big picture and see how marketing, finance, and accounting interrelate with one another and with the pending sale at hand. By understanding these interrelationships, the salesperson with a competent business knowledge will be able to create sufficient customer value so that the customer will be willing to pay more (see Sales Traps 12 and 13).

SALES BEHAVIOR THAT CREATES VALUE

Whether customers see value in a sales offering can often be traced to the behavior of the salesperson (and his or her management). As Sales Trap 11 explains, top sales performers create value, they don't just communicate it. Some people think that they create value when they really don't. Sales Traps 9 through 18 are examples of the mistaken beliefs and partial truths that these salespeople hold. Because they don't fall into Sales Traps 9 through 18, top performers create value from the customer's perspective, and so they generate more sales than average performers. In order to excel at creating value, salespeople need to hone their sales skills (especially their probing skills). They need to figure out the real issues that their clients face. Clients may not be able to communicate their real concerns. The consultative salesperson needs to help the client articulate these concerns by probing deeply and conveying an understanding of the issues. One senior executive of a multinational corporation said it well: "We want to hire the best, develop the best, and be the best. I have always believed you have to try harder to stay ahead, not try harder to get ahead."

*   *   *

sales trap 9:
You Won't Make the Sale Unless You Reach the Decision Maker

For years, salespeople have been taught that to make a sale, they have to reach the decision maker (the person with power, usually at the top of the organization). That's a fallacy based on the wrong information.

THE PROBLEM WITH GOING TO THE TOP

There's no value created by going to the decision maker. Value creation comes from understanding the customer's needs on both a day-to-day level and a global level. Let me explain what I mean. If an enterprising young sales consultant attempts to secure an appointment with the president of a company to sell a piece of office equipment, he or she is misdirecting the sales effort.

Of course the president is consulted when the company buys equipment. But generally this kind of day-to-day decision involves factors that the president isn't knowledgeable enough about to enable him or her to make the decision. He or she will defer the responsibility to the staff. (Even if the president were knowledgeable, he or she probably wouldn't make a decision without first consulting with the staff.)

The people who work with the office equipment every day are the ones who have the problems the equipment is intended to solve. They're in the best position to determine the benefits of a product. Because they're the ones who will get the most value out of the new equipment, the salesperson should focus first on them, not on the president. If the president is against purchasing equipment for financial reasons (the *global* view), the salesperson will have to address that. But the president is not the one with the everyday understanding of the problems (the *day-to-day* view). To create value, salespeople would be wiser to invest their time visiting with the staff members who will actually use the products or services every day.

Let's take another example. A consultant discussing sales training issues with the president of a multibillion-dollar company should not expect him or her to have in-depth knowledge of the specifics, such as the sales skill modules. Nor should the consultant expect him or her to be aware of the merits of one particular program relative to another. Senior managers within a company tend to function as strategists with a global view, not as tacticians. They view their division or their company from 100,000 feet. Since senior managers need to work in a team atmosphere with the people who have the view of the problem from 10 feet, it is highly irregular for any senior manager of a medium-size or large company to make a unilateral decision without consulting and conferring with these people.

WHAT WORKS BETTER

A more effective strategy for managing the decision process within the account is to develop breadth and depth. *Depth* means a detailed understanding of the customer's needs and concerns—that is, a detailed understanding of the problems faced by the people who view them from 10 feet away. *Breadth* refers to the *global* view from the customer's perspective, an understanding of the "big picture" concerns that keep senior managers in the account up at night. An excellent salesperson is able to provide solutions at both the breadth and depth level. Salespeople who master the breadth and depth strategy manage the decision-making hierarchy more effectively, which creates value.

Sales researcher Neil Rackham refers to the need for salespeople to develop needs at three levels in the account:

△ *Focus of receptivity:* These are the person(s) within the account who are willing to meet with you.

△ *Focus of dissatisfaction:* Referred to as the "users," these are the people with the day-to-day problems to be solved.

△ *Focus of power:* These are the decision influencers and decision makers.

When you meet with the people who are at the focus of dissatisfaction, the idea is to "find a sponsor who will either introduce you to or represent you at the focus of power." Rackham goes on to caution the sales consultant not to be discouraged "if your sponsor will not let you meet directly with the decision-maker."[1]

It is not always necessary for you to be able to schedule a meeting with a decisionmaker; it can be just as effective to have someone else to schedule that meeting for you. Besides, in a large and complex sale, there is probably no such thing as one decision maker.

Here's a story that serves as an example of this.

A friend of mine, Steven, had a university-oriented project that he knew would interest the chancellor of a Midwestern state university (focus of power, focus of dissatisfaction). Steven was unable to set up a meeting with the chancellor. He had written letters and made telephone calls, with no results, and he had contacted almost everyone he knew.

Steven asked me if I knew the chancellor. I didn't, but I knew an associate dean (focus of receptivity) and called him. The associate dean told me that he didn't know the chancellor well, but that he played racquetball with a friend named Ted, who was a direct report to the chancellor (focus of receptivity, but possibly also focus of dissatisfaction and focus of power).

I asked the associate dean to arrange a meeting between Ted (the direct report to the chancellor) and my friend Steven. The associate dean set it up. When Steven met with Ted, he probed to assess Ted in terms of his being a focus of receptivity, focus of dissatisfaction, and focus of power. Ted turned out to be a diamond in the rough. He not only believed that Steven offered a solution that created value for the university, but also offered to set up a meeting of the chancellor, himself, and Steven to discuss the project. From there, the sale proceeded well for Steven.

ACTION POINTS

→ *Not reaching the decision maker doesn't mean failure.* What's important is that the decision maker is presented with your ideas in a concise and articulate manner. You don't always have to be the messenger.

→ *Develop other relationships within the account.* Develop relationships with people in the account who are receptive to your approach or knowledgeable about the problems the product may solve. Wide and deep relationships within the account are useful, since people and positions change over time.

SALES TRUTH 9: Develop other areas in the account and let them influence the decision maker.

---

sales trap 10:
Rank Decision Criteria Relative to Competitors

Many salespeople believe that you need to identify and rank the customer's decision criteria. This is a fallacy that misses the mark in creating value for the customer. Just because the customer ranks your offerings as stronger than your competitors' according to certain criteria does not mean you will get the business. *What matters is whether the areas in which you're stronger are the areas that the customer ranks as the most important.*

AN EXAMPLE

> Three banks, Bank 1, Bank 2, and Bank 3, are competing for a lending project. Bank 1 is perceived by the client to be strong relative to the competition in terms of rate, flexibility, and reputation. (Banks 2 and 3 are perceived as weaker on these three criteria.) But what happens if rate, flexibility, and reputation aren't important to the customer? Let's say, for instance, that what really matters to the client is the loan officer's expertise and the bank's expertise. If this is the case, then Bank 1 may very well lose the business to Bank 2 or Bank 3 if Bank 1 is perceived as weaker in loan officer's expertise and bank expertise, since these are the areas that matter most to the client.

SALESPEOPLE DON'T ASK CUSTOMERS TO RANK CRITERIA

My field observation studies reveal that sales consultants normally do not ask the customers how they rank their decision criteria. They should. Questions that they need to ask include:

△ Which criteria are most crucial?

∆ Which criterion is most critical?

∆ Which are desirable?

∆ Which are relatively unimportant?

Even when the salespeople ask for this information, only 18 percent of the time do they ask the customer to make comparisons and indicate which critical criterion is more important than other critical criteria.[2]

WHY IDENTIFYING CRITERIA ISN'T ENOUGH

The standard advice given to salespeople has been to identify the criteria upon which the customer will base the decision. In addition, some managers recommend that these decision criteria should then be prioritized.

This advice is faulty because it is based on two wrong inferences.

TRADING OFF ONE CRITERION FOR THE MOST IMPORTANT. The first wrong inference is that the customer knows how to prioritize the criteria. Often customers don't think formally about how they rank criteria. Therefore, you have to get them to think about it by asking questions such as, "Which one of these two criteria, delivery or price, is the most important?" One critical decision criterion may be more important to the customer than another critical criterion. In other words, customers may be forced to trade off one critical criterion for another because only one solution provider can meet their number-one criterion.

OMITTED CRITERIA. The second wrong inference is that the customer will use all critical criteria in the decision-making process. In fact, the customer may omit a critical decision criterion from the decision-making process. For instance, the customer may not be able to distinguish among the various competitors on the criterion of service.

Therefore, the customer will not be able to use this criterion in making a final decision—not because it isn't important to the customer (it is), but because the customer doesn't see how it will help in selecting between the competing alternatives. It's not objective. Rackham refers to these types of criteria as "soft" in his book *Major Account Sales Strategy.*

DIFFERENTIATING OFFERINGS

If customers can't see a criterion as objective, they can't use it to differentiate the sellers' offerings. Subjective criteria, by definition, are difficult to measure. Therefore, in addition to understanding how a customer ranks the critical decision criteria, the consultant must help the customer to quantify the subjective criteria. Don't just rank the criteria; make the criteria objective.

If the customer can't quantify service, for example, he or she may exclude it from the decision-making process. What does the customer mean by service? Is it measured by the number of hours it takes the loan officer to return telephone calls? Or by the number of invoicing errors? Is it measured by the frequency of visitations?

It's not enough to identify and rank the customer's decision criteria, because the customer still may not be able to use the results. Sellers need to be able to demonstrate their ability to meet an *objective* critical decision criterion that the competitor can't meet. This entails turning subjective critical criteria into objective criteria.[3] Customers need decision criteria that they can use to distinguish or discriminate between the various competing options. They favor objective, measurable decision criteria.

Objectivity sells better to customers' superiors and subordinates than subjectivity—at least if you can provide factual evidence. While there may be some feeling and judgment left in any subjective criterion, the salesperson should quantify the criterion as much as he or she can.

CRITERIA ARE IN THE EYE OF THE BEHOLDER

Jan Carlzon defines any interaction a customer has with your company as a "moment of truth." Moments of truth, like beauty, are in the eye of the beholder and can be almost anything. Jerry Fritz, director of sales and customer service management programs for the Management Institute at the School of Business at the University of Wisconsin–Madison, says, "A moment of truth is when an airline passenger pulls down her seat-back tray to find a coffee stain and infers that the airline is sloppy about engine maintenance."[4] Moments of truth are customer perceptions of value. They are subjective. So are buyers' decision criteria. Decision criteria, as defined by one of my colleagues, are "those important factors which customers use to evaluate, compare, and choose between the options that are available to them."[5] Decision criteria vary from customer to customer, and a criterion that is crucial to one customer may be much less important to another.[6]

Customers are increasingly looking inward for their decision criteria. Their concerns focus more on themselves, their boss, and the competitive issues they face than on their own customers. For example, they see it as OK to define service in terms of how it affects them, the buyers, and they fail to consider how it affects their customers. Decision criteria now include their responsibilities to themselves and to their stakeholders (employees, stockholders, customers, etc.).[7]

OBJECTIVE AND SUBJECTIVE CRITERIA

It's helpful to divide decision criteria into two types: objective and subjective. As discussed previously, these terms refer to whether a particular decision criterion is measured quantitatively (objectively) or qualitatively (subjectively) by the customer. Common subjective criteria that are not necessarily industry-specific include:

△ Reputation

△ Flexibility

△ Convenience

△ Accountability

△ Service

△ Dependability

△ Reliability

△ Customer service

△ Industry expertise

△ Quality

Objective criteria that apply to many industries include:

△ Price

△ Rate

△ Fees

△ Size

△ Payment terms

△ Contract length

△ Specific terms and conditions

△ Warranties

△ Speed

△ Paper capacity

△ Guarantees

STEPS TO CONVERT SUBJECTIVE CRITERIA TO OBJECTIVE

The consultative salesperson should use a three-step process to convert subjective criteria into objective, measurable ones.

1. *Seek the customer's definition.* Ask the customer to define a particular criterion. For example, you might ask, "Allison, what do you mean by service?" or "How do you define service, Allison?" Listen for things that are measurable or specific. The customer's definition of service might be defined as four hour response to service calls or pages. Four hours is specific and objective. It can be measured. Hopefully, it's an expectation you can meet.

2. *Quantify the customer's definition.* If the customer doesn't offer any specific definition that can be measured, then you might offer one. For example: "Emily, you felt service was critical in your decision process. Would a 98 percent up-time on this product meet your standard for excellent service?"

3. *Find out how critical these new quantified criteria are to the customer.* Once a subjective criterion has been objectified, the salesperson needs to know where it is on the customer's priority scale. For example: "Emily, you stated that 98 percent up-time would be considered excellent service, but tell me, is this 98 percent availability more important than price, or is it less important?"

Neil Rackham's research established that people basically go through three steps when they make a decision to evaluate a solution:

1. They list their decision criteria.

2. They prioritize their criteria.

3. They select the alternative that meets these decision criteria the best.[8]

Salespeople need to keep the third step in mind. Salespeople create customer value by identifying how the customer measures the decision criterion and then ensuring that the seller's solutions meet these criteria better than competitors' solutions.

ACTION POINTS

→ *Ask buyers what their decision criteria are.* Some people may not have thought through their criteria. Experts are more likely to be able to answer this question than first-time buyers. Many salespeople forget this step.

→ *Discover how the customer ranks the criteria on a critical to irrelevant scale.* Ask, ask, ask.

→ *Explore the reasons for the customer's ranking.* Customers will often change their criteria before they make a decision, so it's important to know why a particular criterion is of value to them. Value and benefit questions are helpful here. For instance: "Why is 98 percent up-time so important and critical to your operation? Why is four-hour response time key?"

→ *Transform subjective criteria into objective criteria.* Remember the three steps in converting a subjective criterion into an objective one: Ask the customer to define the criterion, ask about other "measurables" that you know could be used, and ask how important this new definition is to the client. Assist the customer with your own ideas for measurement. (It's always helpful if you ask the customer, rather than stating measurement criteria). For example: "Could you or do you measure quality in terms of *Consumer Reports* rankings?" Find out how the customer compares this new definition of the subjective criterion against other critical criteria.

For example: "Is the fact that *Consumer Reports* magazine ranks our product #1 in quality and value more important to you than the fact it is X dollars more expensive than product Z?"

SALES TRUTH 10: Satisfy customers' decision criteria *the way they rank them* to differentiate your offerings.

---

sales trap 11:
Providing Information About Products and Services Creates Customer Value

Salespeople are sadly mistaken if they think that by communicating information about products and services—such as new pricing, new discounts, and product data—they are creating value. That's a fallacy based on outdated market information and old research. These days, customers can get this information from the Internet. Current research shows that concentrating on information causes the seller to focus too much on solutions and not enough on customer problems, needs, and concerns.

WALKING BROCHURES

I call salespeople who give too much information "walking brochures." We've all been approached by the salesperson who dispenses a lot of information and talks *at* the customer, not *with* the customer. The following exchange is between John, a consultant with Solar Systems Solutions, and Andria, the manager of information systems at World-Tech. John is calling on Andria and hopes to sell her a new software package that Solar Solutions has recently developed.

> *John (Consultant):* Andria, you are going to be excited about a new product that we launched fifteen days ago. You asked me nine months ago if I thought we were going to bring something to market that would integrate the hardware and software from your manufacturing, marketing, and accounting departments. Well, we are going to be introducing this solution to the marketplace on May 1. Apparently, our beta-test results have exceeded our own expectation levels.
>
> Let me tell you all the things it will be able to do for you. (*A twenty-minute monologue ensues, in which John provides Andria*

with all the test results and tells her how this new software will
help her improve the communication effectiveness between her
departments.)

Andria: *(as John has to stop talking to take a breath of fresh air)*
John, how much does this cost?

John: Well, it is not all that much when you consider what it
will do for you. For example, just think about how quickly the
marketing organization will be able to update your sales force
regarding pricing changes. Because of this rapid notification
process, your customers will not be claiming that they weren't
notified about price increases. Moreover, . . .

Andria: *(now she needs to interrupt John)* John, how much do you
estimate that your solution will cost us?

John: Oh, approximately between $1.3 and $1.5 million, but the
value you will be getting will more than offset this price. Let
me tell you about another benefit of our product that I hadn't
mentioned. . . . *(John continues to ramble for another ten minutes.)*

Andria: John, as you say, there sounds like there is some value
in your new product, but it doesn't have that much value to
me. Thanks for stopping by.

John: But . . .

Andria: Good-bye, John!

Salespeople like John think that by communicating information,
such as new pricing, new discounts, and product data, they are creating value. Most of the prospect's and the seller's time spent dis-
pensing information in this way is simply wasted. Salespeople who
focus on the product or service they're offering are not learning
what "value" means to the customer.

Here's another example: The Dartmouth Group, Ltd., has observed that sales reps who call on physicians tend to function as talking brochures, i.e., they give rather than seek information. Probably because they have industry expertise themselves, these "doctor reps" spend too many minutes of the sales visit *telling the doctor why his or her patients will benefit from a new product* instead of probing to uncover the doctor's needs. Dr. Richard Ruff of Sales Momentum in Scottsdale, Arizona, says, "In general, salespeople seem to be able to spend more time with doctors in sales calls when they ask really good questions and keep the doctor involved in the dialogue. Asking good questions enable the reps to identify opportunities for them to create value for the doctors."[9]

NEW PRODUCT LAUNCHES

Another opportunity to create value for themselves, their companies, and their customers that salespeople miss comes about when new products are introduced or launched. Research has shown that salespeople who focus more on their new product aren't as effective as salespeople who focus more on the customer's needs.[10] Salespeople normally are excited about new products and can't wait to tell their customers all about them. However, there is a danger. As Neil Rackham, the eminent sales researcher says, "My research showed not that skepticism was better or that enthusiasm is bad; just that enthusiasm can make the seller focus on products, solutions, and answers, rather than on customer problems, needs, and issues."[11] Salespeople should not "let enthusiasm get in the way" of focusing on customer concerns.[12] This can be very difficult for salespeople in the beginning. If they offer their demonstrations and solutions later in the sales cycle, after they have thoroughly explored their customer's needs by asking more good business questions, they are more likely to make a sale.

ACTION POINT

→ *Don't let enthusiasm get in the way of creating value.* Focus on customer needs by asking lots of really smart questions instead of giving information in order to create value.

SALES TRUTH 11: Salespeople need to create value, not communicate value.

---

sales trap 12:
You're Selling Value Versus Price

Have you ever heard any of these comments before?

1. *"It's hard for us to sell value. We're the high-priced provider."*

2. *"We're the biggest in our industry, so we're the leader in price."*

3. *"Customers buy on price now. We're not the lowest-priced player in the market, so we lose a lot more business than we should."*

4. *"Why doesn't the company wake up? It's not 'the economy, stupid!' it's 'the price, stupid!'"*

Every one of these comments is based on the price-value fallacy. The price-value fallacy defines value in the seller's terms, not the customer's. These comments are based on the faulty inference that salespeople have to trade off price and value *when they really don't.* Worse yet, comments 2 and 3 are examples of how salespeople let their companies define the value for customers.

VALUE IS IN THE EYE OF THE BEHOLDER

Value varies by customer. Companies seem to recognize that some of their salespeople don't generate value for their customers, but these same companies often don't recognize that they may be partly responsible for this when they get their sales force hyped up about value. As the old saying goes, "Beauty is in the eye of the beholder." Similarly, "Value is in the eye of the customer."

Perhaps the single biggest challenge for salespeople is to persuade a prospective customer to pay a premium price for the goods or services they're selling. Most customers will not pay a higher price for a product unless they perceive that the value outweighs the price. Unfortunately, many customers do not see the added value that justifies the price.

Why do some customers see the added value in a particular product while other customers don't? Often this difference can be traced to the behavior of the salesperson. Let's examine a relatively common sales scenario.

> The buyer for ISP Co. has indicated that he needs a proposal and that it should include the "best price" possible. Sally, the salesperson from Router & Switcher, asks the buyer a few questions, then returns to her office to put together her proposal. A few days later, Sally delivers the proposal. The buyer tells her he'll get back to her shortly. She asks the buyer what he thinks of the proposal, and the buyer replies that Router & Switcher's price seems relatively competitive. A few days later, Sally learns that a competitor has been awarded the order. And, sure enough, that competitor had a lower price.

The scenario in the preceding example is all too common. Some salespeople blame their employer in this situation because they don't feel their firm's products are price-competitive. Other salespeople complain that their marketplace is now commodity-driven and that their company's products are not different enough to justify the higher price tag. Management thinks the problem is that many of their salespeople can't sell very well. They point to the fact that 20 percent of their salespeople win more of these competitive situations than the remaining 80 percent do. So who's right?

Consider another example.

> Heather, an office products consultant, has just completed her third sales visit with Jason, the chief financial officer of Omnitech. During this visit, Heather learned that there was only one competitor that had a lower price, and that that competitor's product didn't

stack up as well as hers. Heather was feeling relieved and excited—so excited, in fact, that she called her boss and told him that she felt the company would be receiving the $1 million contract by the end of the quarter. He also shared in Heather's excitement. Who wouldn't? You can do everything the customer wants. You have the lowest price. It's in the bag, right?

Wrong!

A few weeks later, Jason had to inform Heather that she didn't receive the business. Jason told her that it came right down to the wire. Although Heather's proposal was less expensive than that of the company Omnitech had selected, and although it seemed to Omnitech that there were no appreciable differences between Heather's proposal and her competitor's, Omnitech felt that Heather's implementation process was not as detailed as that of her competitor. At the end of the day, Omnitech was concerned with the risk, effort, and hassle that it perceived might be associated with implementation issues. These issues ran the gamut from morale, equipment downtime during implementation, and the personal concerns of each of the members of the task force that it might reflect on them if the implementation did not go smoothly.

DISTINGUISHING PRICE AND COST

What went wrong? Heather did not distinguish between price and cost. Unfortunately for Heather, her customer did. Customers view price as a subset of cost, if not always consciously, then at least subconsciously. They perceive price as only *one* factor of cost. Other factors are:

△ The hassle of changing suppliers, vendors, or partners because of the time it will take to get to know all the new people on the scene

△ The effort it will take switch suppliers in terms of time demands on the customer

△ The risks associated with making a change, such as contractual conditions or political issues within the account

"If you think a large, complex sale is going to be *too easy*, it is more likely to be *too hard*," cautions Mike Navel, a training consultant who works with a large pharmaceutical company. And, sure enough, Heather lost the business to a competitor whose price was 7 percent higher than hers.

PROBING FOR RISKS

In order to avoid the situation Heather found herself in, salespeople should probe for other cost issues. Is the buyer concerned that your firm is a new manufacturer? (Risk relating to the reputation or performance of the seller.) Is the buyer bothered that the product looks so complicated that it will take too long to learn how to use it? (Risk relating to the buyer.) Is the buyer concerned that the buyer's staff might never be able to learn how to use it? (Effort and hassle for the buyer's staff and career risk for the buyer.)

Other examples of risks are:

△ Career risks to the client if the decision turns out poorly

△ Product risks to the company if the product fails to live up to its claims

△ Emotional risk associated with poor prior experiences with a company

△ Technology risk that the "new technology" will not be mainstream two or three years from now

△ Loyalty risk, in that a customer may feel disloyal if he doesn't give the business to his *friend*

Interestingly, although customers often say that price was the reason they went with a competitor, in many cases the real reason was some other risk factor.[13]

PRICE DOESN'T EQUAL COST

What could Heather have done differently? She could have recognized that toward the end of the decision process, customers begin to weigh risks other than just price against the benefits and value. Heather should have probed for these risks rather than focusing on price. She could have asked questions such as:

△ Are there any particular concerns or issues besides price that might factor into your decision that I haven't addressed or answered satisfactorily?

△ Are you totally comfortable with our implementation strategy?

△ Do you see any particular political barriers that might prevent us from getting the business?

△ Does our new technology raise any concerns in your mind regarding its effectiveness or its leading-edge benefits?

To summarize, value is your solution's benefit offset by its total cost, *as defined in the eye of the beholder, the customer.* Therefore, salespeople who want to create value would do well to (1) investigate and explore their customer's needs thoroughly, and (2) ask about potential risks, other than price, later in the sales cycle.

ACTION POINTS

→ *Sell value versus total cost, not value versus price.* In the value-versus-cost equation, price is a subset of cost. It's important to determine which costs are important to the customer. Ask the customer about perceived risks, extra effort, or hassles if the customer moves ahead with the buy decision.

→ *Sell the decision criteria.* The salesperson should ask the prospect to define and agree to objective and measurable decision criteria in such areas as service, reputation, expertise, convenience, dependability, quality, image, productivity, responsiveness, flexibility, and relationship. (For a full discussion, see Sales Trap 10, "Rank Decision Criteria Relative to Competitors.")

→ *Help customers distinguish between price and cost.* Today's customers look at total cost, including both direct and indirect costs. The correct way for salespeople to look at price is to see it as one of many factors the customer perceives. Other factors include benefits, savings, and solutions on one side, and hassle, risks, effort, extras, and price on the other.[14]

SALES TRUTH 12: You're selling value versus perceived total cost.

---

sales trap 13:
Lower Your Price to Make the Sale

Real estate agents say that value in real estate boils down to location, location, location. Salespeople say value in selling boils down to price, price, price. In reality, it's usually not necessary to lower the price. Unfortunately, salespeople aren't sure what to do when the customer says, "I can't buy because your price is too high." They believe that the price is in fact too high, not that they didn't create enough value, and thereby fall into this sales trap. They lower the price.

There's a great temptation to lower the price to close the sale, but that leads to sellers losing value. Are salespeople right to lower prices? When customers say it's price, is it really? Actually, no. Research has shown that almost two-thirds of the time the customer tells the salesperson that price is the reason for not buying, price is not the compelling reason.[15]

Here's an example:

> Jennifer, an architect for Boards & Lumber, has bid on the job to design the new corporate offices of Thunder Bay Limited, to be located in Vancouver, British Columbia. She is expecting to get the go-ahead from David, the senior vice president of operations at Thunder Bay Limited.
>
> As Jennifer sits down in David's office, she is anxious but optimistic. But then she hears those dreaded words "Jennifer, I have some bad news. We decided to go with Able & Abler as our architectural partner. It's nothing personal, you understand, just business. Their price was 12 percent less than yours," says David.
>
> Jennifer is almost speechless. "David, if we were to reduce our price, would you re-evaluate your decision?" she asks.

"Unfortunately, our decision is made. I know how you must feel. But everybody's looking at ways to get better prices today, so this is just another cost reduction decision. I hope you understand. At any rate, good luck. As you know, Jennifer, you win some and you lose some." And, with that said, Jennifer is dismissed with a shake of the hand.

As you might expect, Jennifer is beside herself. She can't wait to get back to her office and read the riot act to Lumber's executive vice president, Vince Carrabba, whom she had warned that her proposal to Thunder Bay was "too pricey."

"Vince, I told you so. You guys wouldn't listen, would you? David told me that price was the reason we didn't get the contract. Some days this whole place just makes me mad. I have to take a break."

Jennifer proceeds to her office and calls Cameron, her colleague at the firm. She asks him to meet her for lunch so that she can emote. At lunch she says, "Cameron, do you realize that for the last three years I have been earning less money each year because of our prices?"

Cameron, who hasn't been losing much business because of pricing—who has, in fact, increased his personal earnings substantially year after year—asks Jennifer, "Have you ever thought it might be something that you aren't doing or should be doing that is causing you to lose so often on price? Have you considered that the customer may have needs other than price that you haven't explored fully? You can't always count on people to tell you everything, Jennifer. You may want to reevaluate your probing techniques."

"Cameron, you're starting to sound like Vince, so quit it. My customers are just flaky," she retorts.

IS PRICE THE PROBLEM?

In the above scenario, could Jennifer have been having a *value* problem? I think so. As Tom O'Neil, president of Office Works (a distributor for one of the world's premier office furniture manufacturers), says, "In today's business world, our customers are looking for the best value. If our salespeople cannot create value for their customers, then why should we expect one of our customers to pay a higher price for a similar product or service that one of our competitors offers?"

I believe that Jennifer probably lost the sale because she did not distinguish her offering from those of her competitors. Customers will then take the lowest-price offering *when they don't see any difference between products.* Price isn't the problem. Price is the symptom of a deeper problem. "Price is a polite way of bringing up other concerns," Neil Rackham says. "In the later stages of a complex sale, a price objection may signal an unresolved consequence for the buyer. The salesperson should help the customer identify those concerns and worries, but can't solve them. Only the buyer can do that."[16]

CONSEQUENCE ISSUES

Let's look at Jennifer's example again.

In Jennifer's case, David's unspoken "consequence" issue may have been that Jennifer's company, Lumber & Board, was a new company (only five years old) and its competitor, Able & Abler, was much more established (over thirty-five years old). David may have feared that Lumber & Board didn't have the proven track record, experienced staff, or creative ideas staff to handle the demanding project. Reducing the price will do nothing to resolve any of these consequence issues.

Sometimes the real issue is price. But before you start to negotiate price, follow these three steps first.

STEPS BEFORE NEGOTIATING PRICE

1. INVESTIGATE THE CLIENT'S DECISION CRITERIA. Find decision criteria that not only are important to the client but also can help the client separate your offerings from your competitors'. Remember, it's not what you perceive the criteria and differences to be, but what the client perceives.

Ask yourself if your customer will be able to measure or determine which decision criteria you meet better than, as well as, or worse than your competition. Will the decision criteria that the client is using permit him or her to distinguish among the options effectively?

For example, the customer may feel that product quality is important. Since quality is a subjective characteristic, the salesperson needs to make sure that the client can determine which of the competing product solutions is superior with respect to quality. How does the customer measure the quality difference among the various options? You may have to provide the client with some quantifiable standards used to measure quality.

Describing the decision criteria in terms of measurable, objective standards is important because customers are more comfortable using objective criteria. If your definition of quality is better than your competitors', then the customer will be more likely to use your definition. If the customer can't distinguish between alternatives because a criterion is too subjective, he or she is not likely to use that criterion when making the final decision.

In Jennifer's case, the client was interested in experience. Jennifer didn't explore the definition of experience with David. She accepted the definition that experience meant years the company had been in business. Lumber & Board was a new company (only five years old), and its competitor Able & Abler was much more established (over thirty-five years old). But wouldn't David have been interested to know that Jennifer's executive vice president, Vince, had thirty-three years' experience in drafting corporate center designs and that three of his designs had won national awards? The dialogue might have gone something like this:

Jennifer: I understand that experience is crucial in your decision process. Just what do you mean by experience?

David: Basically the number of years that a company has been in business.

Jennifer: Well, that sure makes sense. When you say "number of years a company has been in business," does that include individuals within the company?

David: Well, yes.

Jennifer: Wouldn't you also want to know the experience levels of the people who will be working on your project? Like how many years of experience they have, how many corporate centers they have designed, how many awards for design they have won?

David: Of course, those are important issues also.

In this example, Jennifer did two things:

1. She asked David his definition of experience: "Just what do you mean by experience?"

2. She inquired if other factors relating to experience were also important: "Wouldn't you also want to know the experience levels of the people who will be working on your project? Like how many years of experience they have, how many corporate centers they have designed, how many awards for design they have won?" These factors would have helped to differentiate her company from its competitor.

If Jennifer had explored David's definition of the experience criterion, she might have won the sale.

2. LOOK FOR RISKS OTHER THAN PRICE. The second step is to ask yourself, *are there other risks to the customer besides price?* You need to identify, reduce, or eliminate any risk you can to help keep price out of the discussion. That will help you avoid lowering the price if you don't have to. While the customer is comparing the various offerings against his or her decision criteria, ask questions about what he or she sees the risks to be in choosing your solution.

If the prospect measures risk in some quantifiable way—for example, in terms of price, penalties, or delivery terms and dates—you may have to enter into negotiations to resolve the customer's specific concern. However, before you negotiate, see whether resolution of these particular concerns will result in an order. (Again, this is so you won't lower the price when it isn't necessary.)

For example, you might ask the customer, "If it weren't for our price compared to that of our competitor, would you select us?" In other words, Jennifer should have asked, "David, is price the only thing keeping you from choosing Lumber & Board?"

The buyer may have other, deeper issues that need to be resolved, such as:

Δ A wrong decision could affect my career.

Δ The seller has a history of poor postsale performance.[17]

Addressing these issues by lowering your price is solving the wrong problem. Dr. Fred Webster, author of *Market-Driven Management* and professor of marketing at the Amos Tuck School of Business at Dartmouth College, used to say that as businesspeople, the most frustrating business experience we would ever encounter would be the discovery that we had solved the wrong problem.[18]

Negotiation of prices should always be the last thing a salesperson does in the sales cycle.

3. SEARCH FOR CREATIVE SOLUTIONS. Even when you've made sure that the only remaining obstacle to the sale is price, there are still creative ways to avoid lowering it. If Jennifer's problem was truly price, perhaps she could have inserted a performance clause into her proposed contract that would have made David and his staff feel more confident. Other creative examples might include:

△ Providing additional implementation support

△ Stretching payments out over a longer time period

△ Decreasing the up-front retainer money

Top performers use creative solutions to reduce price concerns. Top performers also have the advantage of experience and knowledge of what's possible, especially when it comes to meeting difficult customer requirements. Of course, there are certain requirements that even a top performer can't meet or chooses not to meet. In this case, the salesperson should be candid and honest about saying so.[19]

ACTION POINTS

→ *Identify and develop customer needs.* Ask yourself, "Does the customer view his or her problem as sizable enough to solve?" (For a fuller discussion of this, see Sales Trap 3, "It's Best to Offer Solutions to Problems You See.")

→ *Identify and develop ways to differentiate your offerings from the competition.* Customers can't differentiate among their options unless the criteria they'll use to decide are stated in measurable, quantifiable terms. (This is discussed in Sales Trap 10, "Rank Decision Criteria Relative to Competitors.")

→ *Identify and reduce perceived risks.* Help customers define the perceived risks. Then help them resolve those perceived risks.

→ *Negotiate creatively, but only when you have to.* Avoid negotiating by coming up with creative solutions that don't have a financial impact on the profitability of the sale.

SALES TRUTH 13: You can often make the sale without lowering your price.

> ## sales trap 14:
> # It's Possible to Sell Anything to Anybody

"She can sell ice to Eskimos" is the compliment, meaning that she's a good salesperson. *She can sell anything to anybody* is the idea. This is a fallacy. A salesperson who persuades and pushes won't sell anything at all. If you believe this fallacy, you aren't creating value for your customers.

This fallacy is echoed in a myriad of books on the market, such as *How to Sell Anything to Anybody* by Joe Girard and *You Can Sell Anything by Telephone!* by Gary S. Goodman. In the real world, sales don't go through if the salesperson pushes too hard. It doesn't follow that if you push harder, customers are going to buy more. There's a simple reason for this: The buyer has to need the product or service. In a high-ticket sale, prospects will not buy unless they see value in what you're offering.

PUSHERS AND PULLERS

This sales trap also ignores the analysis of top sales experts, who believe that salespeople come in two basic personality types. "Salespeople come in two types—'pushers' and 'pullers,'" says sales researcher Neil Rackham.[20] Pushers are defined as those salespeople who dump a lot of information on their customers (see Sales Trap 11). Says Rackham, "In the push style, the energy comes from the persuader, who 'tells.' Because the push style is about telling, it's easy to practice and repeat. You get really good at a presentation when you've made it 100 times. So push sellers gravitate to a standard pitch that becomes overpracticed and therefore hard to change. The push style requires power, with expertise or knowledge being a type of power."[21]

In the pull style, on the other hand, the energy comes from the customer through the questions the seller asks. Pullers elicit information from their customers by asking lots of good questions, then customize the solutions around what customers say they need. The pull style takes more time, so it's less suitable for short sales.[22]

PUSH STYLE. Which style works better? The push style works in transactional sales, characterized by:

△ Customer perception that the risk of a wrong decision is low

△ Low purchase price

△ One visit to secure the order

△ Maximum customer coverage at minimum cost

In sales of this type, customers have a casual attitude toward the sale and say to themselves, "So what if my decision turns out bad? I won't lose much money. I won't have invested a lot of time. My decision has no serious or lasting consequences or risks for me." Let's say, for example, that you're approached by a telemarketer to subscribe to a magazine. If you say yes, what will you have lost? $19.95? Five minutes of your time on the phone? Let's say you decide you don't like the magazine. Usually you can cancel immediately without any payment. All in all, your decision is low-risk. People in such situations often buy on impulse—and without needing what they're buying—because the buying decision is small-impact, simple, and low-risk. The push style is perfect for these sales because, although it doesn't create value, this type of sale doesn't require a lot of value.

PULL STYLE. The pull style works well when the total perceived cost is high. (See Sales Trap 12, "You're Selling Value Versus Price.") The pull style works in larger, more complex consultative sales. In such sales, if the salesperson doesn't do an effective job of pulling information from the customer, the value won't appear to offset the cost and no business will be transacted.

One consultant in the high-tech field recommends to consultative software salespeople that they "keep their briefcases shut" until they know what information to offer based on the information they've first pulled from the customer. The consultative method of selling, the pull style, is necessary in today's business world, because a consultative salesperson is only as good as the value she or he can create for customers. Unless she or he creates value, the salesperson serves no purpose that couldn't be fulfilled by less expensive means, such as inside salespeople, customer service personnel, or distribution channels for goods and services.

"Changing from a push style to a pull style can be a challenge to some people. But it is a challenge that they will have to win. In tomorrow's sales world, the era of the salesperson functioning as a 'talking brochure' is over," says Neil Rackham.[23]

Research conducted by John DeVincentes and Neil Rackham predicts a reduction in the number of outside salespeople that companies will use in selling their products, because consultants only add to the cost of doing business.[24] Today's clients don't want to spend money unless they see considerable value in doing so. Consultants who don't know how to create value by thoroughly exploring the customers' needs won't sell much in the future.

ACTION POINTS

→ *Be a puller.* Pullers create the best value for their clients by asking lots of good questions. Pullers have a brighter future in selling than pushers.

→ *Pushers are a dying breed.* Pushers are walking brochures that communicate value instead of creating it. (See Sales Trap 11.)

SALES TRUTH 14: Salespeople come in two types, pushers and pullers, and you can't sell anybody anything unless the buyer has a need for it. Pushers are not as effective as pullers because they don't seek out the customer's needs as well.

---

sales trap 15:
Offer Solutions Early

Here's the conventional wisdom: Don't wait too long before you offer a solution to the customer because the customer will lose interest unless he or she sees the value your solution will provide. This thinking assumes that customers are eager for these solutions, so salespeople must introduce them early in the sales call or sales cycle. If this weren't the case, why should the prospect want to see the salesperson? The conventional wisdom doesn't take into account either real-world experience or research. Some salespeople even offer potential solutions in the opening stage of a sales call or midway through the investigative stage in order to demonstrate that they can be of value to the customer. This is bad.

What's wrong with getting the solutions out early? The salesperson doesn't have a clear sense of whether the solution he or she will offer has sufficient benefit or value to the customer to offset the price the customer will have to pay. The results, as in the following situation, are all too common.

> Chris Carter, a loan officer at Fidelity Federal, a medium-sized southeastern bank, makes a sales call to Princeton Printing Services, a potential client with a growing printing and graphics business. This is Chris Carter's initial visit to Princeton Printing Services, but he knows Pat, the senior manager, from a previous job. The sales call lasts about an hour and a half. Chris asks the following situation-type questions:
>
> What made you decide to get into the graphics business? Why did you select this particular location? Do you have any other partners or investors? What kind of revenues do you expect to be generating five years

from now? Where do you find your customers? Have you benchmarked prices to your main competitors? Who are your main competitors? How long have they been in business? Where are they located? Would you be hiring any of their people? Where would you find people to hire here at Princeton Printing?

Chris then introduces the value of Fidelity Federal's solutions: "You know, Pat, Fidelity Federal has been serving the small business entrepreneur for over thirty-five years now. We offer many products, ranging from cash management services to on-line banking solutions. Most of our customers want more than just a loan. They want other services as well. Let me explain what we can do for you here at Fidelity Federal."

Chris proceeds to describe the various banking services and financing terms and leaves Fidelity Federal materials for Pat to review. At the end of the call, Pat requests some additional materials, which Chris sends right away.

In following up, Chris learns that the customer doesn't see the need for the additional banking services Chris talked about. Pat only wants a loan. "I'm not sure why I didn't sell that account," Chris says. "I thought Fidelity Federal's solution was right for him."

What went wrong?

Chris introduced his value proposition too early in the sales cycle, before he had probed to see how strongly the client needed the additional banking services he was selling. Because the sales call focused on fact and background questions, Chris failed to uncover and develop the customer's needs. He also fell into the sales trap of being a walking brochure, communicating value instead of creating it. (For information on the problems of communicating value, see Sales Trap 11, "Providing Information About Products and Services Creates Customer Value.")

Here's what would have worked better:

> After the pleasantries and after explaining the purpose of the call, Chris asks Pat if he may ask him a few questions. Pat agrees, and Chris begins.
>
> *Chris:* How many other printing locations do you have, Pat?
>
> *Pat:* At the moment, we have three, but by the end of the year we expect to add two more.
>
> *Chris:* I see. Are these three other offices within the city?
>
> *Pat:* No, they are located in rural areas.
>
> *Chris:* Okay. Do you ever have any problems with the deposits from these offices being posted immediately?
>
> *Pat:* Occasionally, there is a delay in our deposits being credited immediately because of posting errors. But, I understand how things like that happen.
>
> *Chris:* I understand. But, tell me, when these deposits aren't posted quickly, does that ever lead to overdrafts?
>
> *Pat:* Yes, that has happened, but I just use my credit line to cover it.
>
> *Chris:* Your solution seems to be to draw on your credit line. So, let me clarify my understanding, does that ever seem to you like you are solving the wrong problem?
>
> *Pat:* Yes, but what choice do I have? I don't want checks to my suppliers to be returned.

Chris: Of course, you don't. But tell me, how would it be helpful to you if you were able to reduce these posting errors and not have to draw on your credit line?

Pat: Well, I guess it would not only reduce my interest costs, but also be less hassle because I wouldn't have to track down the delays and the reasons behind them.

Chris: Would reducing posting errors and eliminating interest charges on your credit line be something that you would like to explore a solution for?

Pat: I admit you have aroused my curiosity. How could you help me?

Chris: Well, Pat, we have a cash management service for those clients who have their loan business with us. . . *(the conversation continues).*

If the value doesn't outweigh the cost, customers won't buy.[25]

ACTION POINTS

→ *"Keep your briefcase shut"* until you're sure the customer sees the value in your solution.[26] Wait until you've figured out how your solution may be more valuable to the customer than your competitor's, so that you can justify your price and the customer can justify the cost.

→ *Does the customer see the value in solving the problem?* If so, what is it? The fact that the customer can't initially think of much value in solving the problem may speak louder than words. It gives you the message that the customer may not perceive the same value that is apparent to you in the solution.

→ *Know when to offer your solution.* Two things must happen first: (1) You should understand the customer's needs thoroughly, and

(2) the customer should recognize the needs as problems he or she wants to solve.

SALES TRUTH 15: Offering solutions later, when you have a better handle on the customer's needs, will improve your chances of making a sale.

---

sales trap 16:
Let the Customer Control the Sales Call

In days gone by, you used to be able to open sales calls with lines like "What are you looking for?" or "What can I do for you today?" Asking the customer to tell you about his or her business is a strategy that will get you into a heap of trouble in today's high-pressure, high-performance sales environment. Customers don't have time to do your research for you. You can get much of this information from annual reports or from databases, saving both of you time. Asking such questions adds no value at all. The idea that the customer should control the sales call is a fallacy.

WHAT CAN GO WRONG

To illustrate what happens when the customer does the talking in the sales call, consider the following example.

> Steve Hillberg, a loan officer, called on a business owner who wanted to expand his packaging business, which was a leader in its industry. This packaging company wanted to add more metal containers to its product line, because it was turning away an estimated $25 million in business each year. Steve's purpose in making the call was to offer creative financial ideas that the company could use to improve its cash flow position while bringing out its new product. Steve also needed to determine whether additional lending opportunities existed.
>
> "Tell me a little bit about your bank," the customer asked. By asking Steve to begin discussing his organization, the customer took control of the conversation. Steve talked enthusiastically about his business for nearly forty-five minutes of the one-hour-and-fifteen-minute call. Steve explained the different divisions of

his bank, ranging from trust and investments to lending and professional services and from E-banking to branch banking. He talked about the new and exciting products and services that his bank had launched in the marketplace over the past year. Unfortunately, Steve didn't learn much about the customer's problems and how he might be able to create value for the customer.

Steve might have been better suited to the role of Wall Street spokesperson for his bank. He was knowledgeable and he was articulate. Unfortunately, at this point in the sales call, he should have been asking the client questions. At the end of the call, Steve knew nothing more about the customer. The sales cycle hadn't advanced at all.

FROM INTRODUCTION TO INVESTIGATION

The first place the sales call can get off track is just where Steve made his mistake. After the introductions are over and the salesperson is making the transition from the introductory stage to the investigative stage, he or she can miss the chance to uncover and develop the buyer's needs. At this point in the sales call, the salesperson should ask the buyer's permission to ask questions. If the salesperson doesn't do this, he or she will soon be in a barrel of trouble, because the customer will control the call with questions and the salesperson won't discover the customer's real needs. Salespeople could say something like:

△ "Do you mind if I ask you a few questions to determine whether I might be of help to you and your organization?"

△ "If you don't mind, I'd like to ask you some questions to see whether you will benefit from my services. Would that be helpful?"

∆ "In order to identify if there is any common ground between our organizations, I'd like to ask you some questions. Would that be okay?"

WASTED INVESTIGATIVE STAGE. Unless the salesperson initiates the investigation, the customer, not the consultant, will end up leading the sales call. If the customer controls the call, the seller may discover too late that he or she hasn't learned anything about the customer's business or needs. The buyer will be less likely to schedule a second meeting, since he or she hasn't any particular reason to meet with that salesperson again. In the words of Frank McKinney Hubbard, "Look out for the fellow who lets you do all the talking."[27]

LEADING THE FOCUS ON CUSTOMER NEEDS. Research by The Dartmouth Group showed that on average, the consultant who guides and leads the conversation during the investigative stage ends up talking less and the client talking more. Generally speaking, customers should be talking more than salespeople, because the focus of the call should be on customer problems.[28]

Here's how Steve could have better handled the sales call. When the customer asked Steve about his bank, Steve should have politely offered a two- or three-minute sound bite. He then should have said something like:

> I could talk for hours about our bank, but in order for me to make certain that I am in a position to create as much value for you as possible, do you mind if I ask you a few questions? This way I'll know a lot better what to tell you and what not to bore you with.

ACTION POINTS

→ *Lead by asking for permission to ask questions.* It's best to ask permission to ask questions early in the sales call. However, there will be additional chances to do this throughout the sales visit when a consultant might want to gain control or focus of the conversation.

→ *Keep the generic information dump brief.* Plan ahead of time what you'll say, if asked. Keep it short.

→ *Focus on information that will link the client's needs to your solutions.* Ask yourself, "Do I know enough about this customer's needs to know what information to give or not give?" Don't offer more information until you do. Keep asking questions until you know which needs the customer has identified as problems to be solved.

SALES TRUTH 16: The salesperson should control the sales call.

> **sales trap 17:**
> ## The Purpose of Questions Is to Persuade Someone to *Do* Something

Salespeople mistakenly think the value in selling comes from persuading customers to buy their product or service. They think that the purpose of questions is to convince someone to do something. These statements are partial truths that lead to Sales Trap 17, which has serious consequences.

In spite of the fact that I've emphasized the power of questions throughout this book, it's dangerous for salespeople to believe that the objective of these questions is to get customers to buy. Don't get me wrong. Without a doubt that's one purpose, but it shouldn't be the main purpose. There has been extensive research to support the fact that good questions are excellent persuaders. This is one point that even today's sales researchers are in agreement on. And the persuasive power of questions is hardly new. It goes back to Socrates. This persuasive power is an axiom. It is truth. It is even fact.[29] But it doesn't paint the whole picture, and salespeople who focus on the persuasive element of questions miss the point that the purpose of questions should be to create customer value.

SELLING ISN'T MANIPULATION

What's wrong with the idea that questions are intended to persuade? It's manipulative. And manipulation has no place in sales, not only because it's unethical, but also because it doesn't work very well compared to other techniques. No one questions the fact that good questions can persuade. However, persuasion is not the most efficient or helpful reason to do business, for either the seller or the customer.

Questions will be perceived as less manipulative if the purpose of the questions is twofold:

1. *Understanding.* One reason to ask questions is to determine whether customers have issues that the seller might be able to help them with. Here, it's important to remember that it's not important that you think the customer has issues you can address; what's more important is what the customer thinks about these issues.[30]

2. *Thinking differently.* A second reason to ask questions is to help someone think differently. Of course, it's possible the other person won't think differently after you've asked the questions. But that's okay, because the primary purpose of asking questions should not be persuasion. Persuasion is merely a result of helping someone to think differently about something. When people set out to be persuasive, they often become combative. Therefore, view persuasion as a reward, not an objective or purpose.

GETTING PEOPLE TO THINK DIFFERENTLY

Dr. Tom Ingram, chairperson of the Marketing Department at Colorado State University, contends that if a salesperson asks questions about the consequences of a customer's business problems, the salesperson is more likely to get the customer to think differently about how serious these problems may be.[31] When questions are asked in order to manipulate, to get someone to do something that he or she may or may not want to do, the strength, honesty, and objectivity of the long-term relationship with the customer is in danger.

Wilson Learning Systems found in its research that in most cases, what passes for consultative selling is simply the needs-based selling approach. Prompting the customer to tell you what he or she already knows is not true consulting. Nor is consulting simply asking questions to determine a customer's needs, listening well to the answers, and recommending the products that best match the customer's stated needs.[32]

Dr. Richard Ruff of Sales Momentum in Scottsdale, Arizona, states:

> The real power of really good questions lies in their ability to cause customers to think about their situation from multiple perspectives. But, of course, asking really good questions is not that simple nor that easy.

EXAMPLE

Harry Harter is a consultant with Ivy Leaguers, a firm specializing in public relations work for athletes. He is calling on Joe Westfall, an agent who represents six of today's tennis stars. Joe recognizes that his athletes don't always project the public persona that he envisions. But he doesn't think this is a big enough problem to warrant paying the premium prices that retaining Harry and Ivy Leaguers would cost until Harry begins asking questions *to try to understand* why Joe didn't think his problem was big enough to solve. The conversation really progresses when Harry continues asking more questions to try to help Joe *think differently* about potential problems that a poor image could cause for the athletes and for Joe himself.

Harry: So, Joe, you are troubled by the image of your tennis stars on and off the court, but you don't feel it's damaging enough to invest in our services right now. In other words, you just don't see the value in a solution at this point, is that right? *(Harry is attempting to make certain he understands Joe's position.)*

Joe: Couldn't have said it better, Harry. I just don't think our players' image problem is a big enough issue to justify spending the kind of money you are asking.

Harry: OK, but what could potentially happen to endorsement revenues as well as your own fees from these revenues if one or two of these players loses his endorsements because of poor media coverage? *(Harry is still trying to understand why this potential problem doesn't bother Joe more.)*

Joe: If it hasn't happened by now, it probably won't happen.

Harry: You don't think it could ever happen?

Joe: Well, if they were going to get into trouble, they would have gotten into trouble by now. It's just that simple.

Harry: That's what Nixon probably thought, too, before Watergate, but he got caught. Are you willing to take the chance that it won't ever happen to your athletes? Can you spare the revenue you would lose? There is no way to predict the future. Isn't the real question here this: Is it better to be safer now than to be sorry later? *(Harry is helping Joe to view his current opinion from a slightly different perspective so that he might think a little differently about it.)*

Joe: Perhaps, but I don't know. Are there any other options besides the one we talked about that wouldn't be as expensive but could reduce my future risk?

Harry: Maybe, but I am going to have to ask you a few more questions first, if you don't mind? *(Harry returns to wanting to probe for understanding.)*

Joe: What do you want to know?

Harry: Well, to begin with, let's examine the status of each contract endorsement by player and try to figure what the financial downside would be if only two of your players lost their smallest endorsements. . . . How much money would we be talking about, Joe?

And Harry continues to try to understand Joe's thought process. As you might expect, Joe began to view the loss of endorsement contracts as a higher risk than he had initially thought. Note that Harry did not even consider *telling* Joe that he could very well have a problem at some point in time. Harry recognized that the value of his services resided in Joe's eyes and not his own.

Persuasion is the end, not the means.

ACTION POINTS

→ *Questions are to understand.* Use questions as tools to help you understand what, why, and how customers think the way they do.

→ *Questions are to change someone's perspective.* Questions are a way of helping someone view a situation differently. But remember, the person may not think any differently immediately after you ask the questions.

→ *Questions cause people to think afterwards.* Questions tend to cause people to think about the answers long after the conversation is over.

SALES TRUTH 17: The purpose of questions is to change someone's perspective and to create value for customers.

---

sales trap 18:
A Skilled Salesperson Doesn't Need to Plan Sales Calls

A lot of people believe that when you get good at sales, you don't have to spend time planning a sales call. You can do it naturally in your head. Or go with your gut.

Is this true or false?

False. It's a mistake to think that you don't have to plan your sales calls. Professional experience and field research proves this point, as I'll show you here.

First, consider the following scenario:

> Mike Bailey, the salesperson from Altix, a high-tech software company, calls for the first time on Sorensen Global Engineering, a prospective client. The sales rep opens his briefcase and demonstrates the cutting-edge, sexy software. The prospect asks how much and gasps at the price. The sale is dead in the water.

Is this an everyday example? You bet. Poor planning often results in poor execution. If they don't plan the sales call, consultants are less likely to learn how they can create value for clients. Mike O'Connor, vice president of corporate accounts for Computer Credit, Inc. (CCI), put the problem this way: "If you don't know where you're headed, any road will take you there. Sales call planning is your road map on how to arrive at value for you and your client." But it is the manager's job to inspect the planning process through her or his inspection, giving feedback and reinforcement.

ASKING TOO MANY SITUATION QUESTIONS

One result of not planning the sales call is that the salesperson seeks too much background or company information that he or she could have acquired from a Dun & Bradstreet listing or annual report. This can bore the customer, who already knows this information. The salesperson needs to seek more information about the customer's issues and needs. Informational questions don't do as much to uncover customers' needs as do other kinds of questions.

Here's an example:

> Steve, a loan officer, called on Phil Campbell, owner of Imago Graphics, a holographic imaging technology business. Since Steve had not spent time preplanning the call, he spent more than an hour and fifteen minutes of his one-hour-and-thirty-five-minute sales call asking the following information-based questions:
>
> Δ How many employees do you have?
>
> Δ Who does your design work?
>
> Δ When do you want to be running?
>
> Δ Have you executed leases on those new machines?
>
> Δ As far as ownership of Imago Partners goes, who's involved?
>
> Δ Is he involved day-to-day?
>
> Δ How do you fit in?
>
> Δ What kind of credit terms will you offer your customers?
>
> Δ Who is your accountant?
>
> Δ Could your equipment needs change?

As you can see, these are mostly factual questions. Because Steve didn't ask any issue-based questions, he was unable to uncover Phil's problems or needs. Nothing was covered that would prevent Phil from shopping around. Valuable time was wasted, and it will take a couple more calls to determine Phil's exact needs and expectations for a financing package—what Steve asked did nothing to uncover that information.

DOING YOUR HOMEWORK

If you want to learn what's on your clients' minds, it's important these days to do your homework. "Tell me about your business," which used to be an acceptable sales opener, now just shows ignorance. "Customers don't want to educate you about their business. Why should they? Good customers have more than enough information about you. They expect you to know as much or more about them," say Kevin Hoffberg and Kevin J. Corcoran.[33]

Here's an example of a preplanned and more effective approach:

> Dave was calling on a customer in the live sound business who had purchased 25 acres and built a 14,000-square-foot building financed through a competing bank. Dave had identified that the purpose of the call was to determine whether there were any needs or expectations that this customer felt were not being met by his current bank. By thinking through the questions he wanted to ask and spending a few minutes thoughtfully writing them out, he developed some really smart questions he could ask regarding issues, concerns, and need development during his one-hour-and-twenty-minute sales call:
>
> △ Can you tell me about the issues you face using your current system?
>
> △ Do you think the issue with collateral will eventually affect your cash flow?

△ At the time, your biggest concerns were getting a Small Business Administration loan and the personal guarantee—which was the bigger concern for you?

△ Did it bother you to give a personal guarantee to your bank?

△ Did the personal guarantee affect your financial condition at all?

△ What other challenges do you have currently? (Problem question)

△ Any other challenges—is your equipment up to the level you need?

△ How comfortable are you with leasing?

△ Can accounting or data entry be a challenge for you?

△ Are there other things, say in the next one to three years, that you envision for which you may need additional financing?

△ And the implications of your having truck problems are . . .?

△ Is that something you'd like us to consider?

△ Did the lender provide you with the flexibility you needed? Is there a way you can see that we can help you do that differently?

△ Do you see any benefits from us being local in the cash management side?

If you are serious about learning what's important, it's better to write down key questions you might want to ask so that you don't forget them during the sales call. Planning the sales call is essential. "Good sellers have plans for territories, accounts, and career paths," says John F. Monoky, president of Monoky & Associates. "For complex, multilevel, long-sales-cycle accounts, they have action plans that identify the specific steps needed over two or three years to capture the business."[34]

ACTION POINTS

→ *Establish the purpose of your call.* What do you expect, anticipate, or know is the reason for the consultative visit? The purpose is what you and the customer will agree upon as the reason why you are meeting; it is normally agreed upon prior to the meeting. For example, the purpose might be to explore ways that we might be able to manage your health care costs more effectively.

→ *Establish your call objective.* What is it that you would like to accomplish during your visit with the customer? It should be something that can be measured objectively. For example, identify at least three client problems and secure a second meeting to explore these three problems more thoroughly.

→ *Write out really smart questions before the call.* Write out the significant information that you will need in order to explore areas that you might be able to help with. Write out questions that will probe into the needs of customers.

→ *Identify the potential impact to the customer of not solving those needs.* If appropriate, don't forget to ask the customer why it is so important to address those needs.

SALES TRUTH 18: Skilled salespeople *do* need to plan their sales calls.

PRINCIPLE

focus on
feedback
and
learning

TOP SALES organizations provide salespeople
with constructive feedback and a healthy learning environment in which they can grow and develop.

FEEDBACK

Feedback is a key factor in a salesperson's development because consultative sales skills are easy in concept, but difficult to execute. Feedback helps the salesperson know which behaviors to change in order to
do a better job. In any sales organization, the most
crucial position when it comes to feedback is the
first-line manager. The manager should see to it that

salespeople get the coaching they need and that they stay focused on the customers' needs. Principle 5 includes several sales traps that managers fall into that adversely affect feedback, and in turn affect salespeople's opportunities to develop:

△ Sales Trap 19, "Sales Skill Training Is Enough to Solve Selling Problems"

△ Sales Trap 20, "If You Generate Sales Activity, You'll Close More Sales"

△ Sales Trap 21, "Top Performers Are the Best Teachers"

△ Sales Trap 22, "Sales Managers Are Good Coaches"

Effective feedback uses the same language as the company's sales-skill training program and also offers an effective sales process for salespeople to follow. Managers should monitor the sales feedback and learning process.

COACHING

Coaching is simple to understand, but difficult to implement. The responsibility for developing salespeople and giving feedback usually rests with the first-line manager. Good managers provide feedback, using the common language of their company's training programs. But feedback alone is not necessarily effective when it comes to sales-skill-based training programs.

It is actually very difficult to find companies in which the first-line sales managers effectively coach the verbal behaviors taught in their company's sales-skill-based programs.[1] Few companies do a good job on this, as is discussed in great depth in Sales Trap 22, "Sales Managers Are Good Coaches."

Many companies struggle to get their sales managers to spend time in skill-based coaching sessions with their reps.

In defense of the first-line managers, there are several reasons why they do not find or take the time to coach, some of which are beyond their control. These reasons include:

△ There is a lack of rewards, recognition, and other incentives that managers can use to develop their salespeople.

△ Job and time pressures from within the company and with clients eat away at valuable coaching time.

△ The selling models are complicated and don't make it easy for managers to coach salespeople or measure their progress.

△ There are conflicts between what the manager believes works and what the particular sales training program states works.

△ Managers fear coaching, either because they don't know how to do it or because they haven't been trained to do it.

In the end, unfortunately, it probably comes down to business priorities, but it's unfortunate that many first-line managers have never even participated in their company's sales-skill-based training program.[2]

As one salesperson put it:

> How can my company expect me to develop my skills as quickly and effectively as they want me to—and as I want to—when my sales manager hasn't even been through the sales skill program we've been using for the last two years? How can he begin to give me feedback on the skills I learned? I know the responsibility for my personal development is primarily mine, but I am jealous of the people who work for managers who know the language in our skill based programs and can offer constructive feedback to my colleagues in the same language.

PERSONAL DEVELOPMENT

Companies that do a good job with feedback and learning place their emphasis on developing a learning culture along with the sales culture. Such companies take steps to see that both cultures flourish. They are committed to their salespeople's personal development. For example, some include "people development" in their managers' annual performance appraisals. A few of the companies that stand out from the rest in this area are Motorola, Northwestern Mutual, and Hewlett-Packard.

Top companies encourage a learning culture by offering financial support for executive education classes, undergraduate degrees, and MBA degrees, and then recognizing educational achievement. Today, most of the *Fortune* 1000 companies, and many other smaller companies as well, offer some form of tuition reimbursement. The best companies tend to offer more attractive and extensive incentives and reimbursements, ranging from monetary reimbursement to career opportunities. This type of commitment sends a message to the sales force: *"We really do care about you and your personal development!"*

*   *   *

---

sales trap 19:
Sales Skill Training Is Enough to Solve Selling Problems

It's a partial truth to say that sales-skill training works (or doesn't work) and that it solves (or doesn't solve) selling problems. It can, but it doesn't necessarily, *unless the sales skills are reinforced.* Research has shown that if you just send reps to training and don't reinforce their skill training, they forget 87 percent of what they learned in the course within thirty days.[3] Sales-skill training, by itself, is not the answer to helping salespeople to learn to sell better. Without continued practice, feedback, and reinforcement by first-line management (or some other experienced coach), the salesperson is unlikely to make much of a behavioral change or improvement.

TRAINING VERSUS REINFORCEMENT

Here, I'm defining sales-skill training as a course, conducted in a classroom, that discusses sales models or the concepts of the selling process. This course is often a discrete training session held in a training or conference room. What I mean by practice, feedback, and reinforcement is face-to-face, real-time practice involving two or more people in which verbal selling behaviors are applied, scenarios are rehearsed, and actual behaviors are modeled and corrected appropriately. Another word for this is coaching. Without feedback and reinforcement, sales reps are unable to translate their knowledge of the sales models or process into more skilled behavior in the sales call.

A PROCESS, NOT AN EVENT

Sales-skill training may improve morale and reduce turnover, but by itself it doesn't produce posttraining improvements in sales results. Many of the organizations that put their salespeople through sales-skill training programs don't achieve the return on their investment that they had hoped for or wanted because they don't reinforce the program afterward. "In most companies, sales training is an event," says Gilmour Lake, president of Computer Credit, Inc., located in Winston-Salem, North Carolina. "[Instead,] it should be an on-going process that is reinforced through coaching."

In fact, coaching makes everyone money, from the company, to the coach, to the salesperson. Knowing and understanding a sales tool is one thing; using it effectively is quite a different story. Sales reps need coaching in order to make this transformation.

POSTCOURSE COACHING

One approach suggested by Learning International (now Achieve-Global) is to redefine sales training to include postcourse coaching. As Achieve-Global points out, coaching is "an individualized development process designed to change a salesperson's behavior to better meet the organization's goals for financial performance and customer satisfaction." And, Achieve-Global argues, "sales coaching is not done in a classroom, nor by accompanying the salesperson on the sales call."[4]

It's hard to "walk the talk." Many sales models are easy to grasp, but hard to execute. Applying those models on the job is time-consuming, difficult, and usually frustrating. Most salespeople are more willing to learn the sales models than to demonstrate them. Human nature dictates that acquiring a new skill that involves changing behavior requires considerable feedback and reinforcement.

ACTION POINTS

→ *Ask for feedback*. Research shows that if sales skill training isn't coached and reinforced, salespeople forget what they've learned. The feedback and reinforcement part of coaching is what drives the return on a company's sales training investment because it's what leads to real behavioral change and improvement by the sales staff. Ask for feedback from your manager, your peers, and your friends when you plan and rehearse sales calls. Without feedback, how will you know whether your sales behaviors are as good as they can be?

→ *Focus on one behavior at a time.* Beginners should focus on one or two behaviors and master those before moving on (see Sales Trap 8, "Beginners Should Start With Comprehensive Training").

→ *Support coaching.* Behavioral change requires coaching. Companies should do more to support coaching. A good coach is just as important in sales as in sports.

SALES TRUTH 19: Sales training *doesn't* work without reinforcement.
----

sales trap 20:
If You Generate Sales Activity, You'll Close More Sales

The following sales management scenario is all too common. A sales force is not achieving its performance targets, and neither is the company. What is the quickest fix? To monitor, inspect, and increase the sales activity levels of the salespeople. From senior management down to first-line management, the mistaken consensus is often that if sales activity levels are increased, an increase in performance will follow. This belief is a fallacy. The conventional wisdom may say that the way to succeed is to "increase your sales activity," but salespeople get themselves into a heap of trouble when they don't distinguish between transactional sales (single visit, low dollar value, low risk) and consultative sales (multiple visits, high dollar value). In transactional sales, salespeople can increase their sales activity by scheduling a sufficient number of appointments, making the required number of sales calls, presenting as many proposals as possible, and performing as many demonstrations as possible.

Salespeople in consultative sales tend to follow the decision process phases of their customers. In a typical decision process, a customer normally passes through three phases. In phase 1, the customer is trying to determine if it wants to solve the problem. In phase 2, after the customer deciding to solve the problem, the customer sets about evaluating the alternative solutions. In phase 3, the customer assesses the risk of the alternative selected in phase 2.

In consultative sales, it is what you learn from customers about their needs that advances the sale, and that comes from quality, not quantity. (Of course, you do need to make sales calls to sustain life. However, it is a strong emphasis upon sales activity in the consultative sale that we are addressing in this sales trap.)

Increasing sales activity works only in transactional sales. In consultative sales, what matters is not how many customers the salespeople see *(quantity)*, but what they say to customers once they're there *(quality)*.

Here's the familiar scenario.

> Ralph, a sales manager for a leading telecommunications company, was reviewing the third-quarter performance of one of his major account reps. "Meredith, it seems that the last ninety days has been particularly tough. You were only at 62 percent of plan, and you're only at 78 percent of plan year-to-date. We need to decide what to do to help your performance improve. Since we only have ninety days left in the year, we need to do something that will get us immediate results. We need you to work harder, Meredith. In other words, we need you to make more sales calls, deliver more demonstrations, and write more proposals. These particular activities will have to generate business somewhere. With increased sales activity levels, Meredith, somebody will stick orders into your pocket. Therefore, let's increase your sales activity levels by 33 percent, and we will review your progress against these activity standards at 7:30 a.m. each Friday morning for the rest of the year. Meredith, you can be sure of one thing. Things will start to happen."

CONSEQUENCES OF THIS SALES TRAP

Things will start to happen, all right. Meredith's performance will probably go down. How can someone work harder and have sales decrease? Because in increasing her activity, she's only skimming the surface of her accounts. She's not learning what her customers need. In the smaller, simpler sale, performance is driven by how many customers the sales rep visits, but in the consultative sale, performance is driven by how effective a salesperson is at learning and listening once he or she is in front of the customer. Therefore, it can be counterproductive to primarily manage sales activity levels for larger, complex sales.[5]

Ted Rubley, former Xerox sales manager and now president of INYFX, says:

> I recognized something early in my sales management career. There seemed to be a difference between how I managed my salespeople who were involved in transactional selling (small sales) compared to my people involved in consultative selling (major accounts). In small sales, I could almost predict that if a rep were making lots of sales calls, he would have lots of orders, too. This didn't seem to hold true with my major account reps, though. They had only so many accounts they could call on. In one sense they couldn't work harder, they could only work smarter. I discovered I was spending more time with them to help develop effective sales strategies and tactics and more time with the transactional reps inspecting activity standard levels.

SALES ACTIVITY DEFINED

Sales activity traditionally has been viewed as particular activities that the salesperson needs to perform in order to be successful.

TRANSACTIONAL SALES. In smaller sales, the following transaction-generating activities will improve sales:

△ Scheduling a sufficient number of appointments

△ Making the required number of sales calls

△ Presenting as many proposals as possible

△ Conducting as many demonstrations as possible

△ Determining a percentage mix between "new business" calls
   and "customer care" visits and then managing to that mix

Sales activity can also include seeking referrals, sending direct
mail to solicit business, following up, and conducting postsale activities. The point is that these activities all work, but they are most
effective in the smaller, transactional type of sale. For example, sales
of small insurance policies, inexpensive office products, personal
pagers, and cellular phones would probably be considered transactional sales. Measuring the number of sales calls, proposals, and
demonstrations works well for selling these products.

CONSULTATIVE SALES. In consultative sales, the salesperson needs to
probe thoroughly and explore the customer issues, the consequences
caused by these issues, and so forth. This takes time. There is much
more for the salesperson to know and understand when she or he is
working with larger accounts. There are more people to visit.
Multiple decision makers are often involved, and working with each
one is time-consuming. In the consultative sale, it's about working
smarter, not harder.[6] It's about learning at a deeper level. When a
salesperson invests much of his or her time with larger accounts
(which he or she should do because the performance reward is usually greater), that salesperson doesn't have as much time left to make
lots of sales calls. In the consultative sale, success is about how the
salesperson behaves in front of the customer, not the number of customers he or she is able to visit. Put another way, in the consultative sale, performance is about depth, i.e., "drilling" down into an
account. In transactional selling, it is about breadth, i.e., calling on
a lot of people. Since the solutions in a transactional sale are usually
not as complex or are more of a commodity, and since they are also
low-risk to the customer, only one or maybe two sales calls are necessary to get an order.

What might happen if a transactional approach were to be used in the consultative sale? Imagine a salesperson who was used to closing business on the first or second visit trying to close an order for a $1.5 million local area network (LAN) order on the same timetable. No one would ever expect a *Fortune* 500 company to move its life, health, and property coverages to the company of a sales rep who tried to close on the second visit. In such cases, the prospect would be thinking, "How could someone who has learned so little about our business be able to make an intelligent recommendation to us? Do we want to do business with someone who doesn't care enough about us to take the time to learn our business?"

Shelby Solomon, vice president and general manager for the MEDSTAT Group in Ann Arbor, Michigan, says, "Of course, we want our major account people making sales calls, but we want them to be effective sales calls. They need to take the time to thoroughly understand the customers' needs and identify how they can create value for our customers."

ACTION POINTS

→ *Consultative sales require quality.* Remember that consultative selling (or major account selling) is about sales effectiveness—in other words, how skilled you are when you are in front of the customer.

→ *Transactional sales require quantity.* In transactional selling, performance is primarily driven by getting in front of a lot of customers, since a high skill level is not necessary for sales success.

SALES TRUTH 20: Increased sales activity is effective only in transactional sales.

---

sales trap 21:
Top Performers Are the Best Teachers

The idea that top performers are the best teachers is a fallacy. It may be clear from watching top performers that they're good. But assuming that *because* they're good they'll be able to teach others is a mistake. It's actually hard to learn from top performers. Here's why.

NOT KNOWING WHY THEY'RE GOOD

We have found that just because top performers are able to "do it" doesn't necessarily mean that they know what it is that they are doing that makes them outstanding. For example, Neil Rackham found that top performers believed that their success came from the category of question they asked (*grammatical form*), when in fact it was the type of question (*purpose*) that mattered.[7]

TEACHING IS DIFFERENT FROM DOING

One reason why top performers aren't necessarily good teachers is that teaching requires a different skill set from doing. When you teach, you are getting others to change their behavior. In self-management, you are getting yourself to change your behavior. The difference is almost the same as that between managing and selling. The skill set for success in management is somewhat different from the skill set used in selling. This is the reason why top salespeople don't always make the best sales managers, and top athletes don't always make the best coaches.

YOU CAN'T JUST WATCH THEM

Some people believe that top performers can teach simply by letting students watch them. If a salesperson could improve by *watching* a top performer, then someone would have filmed a top salesperson, shown the footage to all the beginners in the world, and thus eliminated the need for corporate sales training, sales coaches, and even consultants like me. Verbal skills, such as asking questions, are like physical skills in sports: You have to *practice* new behaviors and get feedback from a coach in order to know how you are doing. Coaching will tell you what to continue doing and what to change. Changing physical or verbal behaviors by reading books and watching instructional movies hasn't worked very well in sports. I don't expect it will work in sales, either. Athletes know that they improve most when they practice and get feedback and reinforcement from their coach.

FIELD RESEARCH WITH TOP PERFORMERS

The Dartmouth Group, Ltd., asked successful salespeople from leading companies throughout the world what they believed the keys to their sales success were and what advice they would pass on to others. Their responses were somewhat varied but almost predictable. Here are some of the more common ones:

△ Ask questions, lots of questions, particularly open-ended ones to get the customer talking.

△ Be persistent and assertive, but not pushy and aggressive.

△ Know your product thoroughly and be able to demonstrate its uniqueness to the customer.

△ Make lots of sales calls.

△ Recognize that some people have it and others don't.

△ Strong interpersonal skills are important in order to be successful.

△ Be honest. The prospect senses it if you're not.

△ Listen for customer needs.

△ Always be closing.

△ Objections are your friend; they will often lead to a sale.

This list offers some interesting insights. First, the responses from top performers were pretty vague. We weren't always certain of what they meant because the context wasn't clear. For example, were there any types of questions within the categories open-ended and closed-ended that were more successful than others? If so, in what situations? Should salespeople believe that they are successful if they are generating lots of objections? Is one type of objection easier or more difficult to handle than another? Second, two of the items on the list, doing lots of closing and generating lots of objections, work better in transactional selling than in consultative selling. (Rackham thoroughly researched this finding and published his study results in *SPIN® Selling*.) Top performers weren't always able to identify the particular conditions under which some sales techniques worked better than others. This kind of person would struggle as a coach.

SUCCESS FACTORS FOR TOP PERFORMERS

The Dartmouth Group, Ltd., has found that:

△ Top performers ask significantly more questions than poor to average performers, and they also ask really smart questions. (See Sales Trap 18, "A Skilled Salesperson Doesn't Need to Plan Sales Calls.")

△ Good salespeople try to gather pertinent information as part of their preparation.[8]

△ Top performers make certain that the customers talk more than they do. They also display concern by seeking and listening more.[9]

△ Top salespeople offer solutions later in the sales cycle, after they have fully explored the client's needs.[10]

△ Top performers place their primary emphasis on "understanding" the customer by asking really good questions.

As you can see, there's a disparity between what top performers said they did and what they actually did. For example, top performers felt that if you could handle objections effectively, you would get sales results. However, the key is to reduce the number of objections by using effective probing techniques. In fact, there were fewer sales objections in successful sales calls than in unsuccessful calls.[11] According to Rick Beller, former vice president of channels for Huthwaite, Inc., and now with the Real Learning Company, "You can learn from the best. You can also learn (what not to do) from the worst, but in the end you learn best from those facilitators and instructors who are the most skilled teachers—and the most skilled teachers may not be the best performers."

ACTION POINTS

→ *In teaching, rely more on research and validated studies than on expert opinions.* Top performers don't always know why they're good, so they aren't the best teachers. For example, in our research, top performers thought that they should be always closing, whereas in the consultative sale, the more closing techniques are used, the less chance there is for sales call success.[12] People who are "students of selling" but are just par or average performers might be better coaches.

→ *Validate the teaching approach.* Don't hesitate to ask any salesperson, sales manager, or sales trainer to validate the teaching approach he or she is using. You might want to ask questions such as, How do you know for sure that what you are suggesting or teaching is correct? What was the research methodology or research database used for your conclusions? For a fuller discussion of courses and methodologies, see Sales Trap 7, "It's the Content of the Skill Training That Matters Most."

SALES TRUTH 21: Top performers don't always know *why* they're the best.

`sales trap 22:`
Sales Managers Are Good Coaches

> Our sales manager is the best coach. As the manager,
> she's in the best position to oversee the day-to-day skill
> development of all of our salespeople through obser-
> vation, feedback, and encouragement.

Does this statement sound familiar? It's a good representation of the common idea that sales managers are good coaches. In point of fact, sales managers are rarely good coaches (though it's through no fault of their own) for the simple reason that *they don't coach*.[13] And without coaching, salespeople don't learn what they need to learn in order to improve.

It's ironic that most managers don't coach because almost everyone agrees on what the attributes of a good coach are, and many sales managers have these qualities in spades. Most people describe a good coach as being skilled, being supportive, and offering feedback.[14] But why don't most people coach effectively if they know what a good coach is?

PEOPLE ASSUME THAT COACHING SHOULD "HAPPEN NATURALLY"
Many organizations do not separate coaching from the sales management function and believe that coaching is supposed to arise naturally from the manager's experience.[15] Most sales managers became sales managers because they were top salespeople. And when they coach, they often want to emphasize the techniques that got them to the top, whether or not those techniques will work in the situation at hand. And the techniques used by sales managers are often outdated. Mike Lockman of The Dartmouth Group says, "Former top salespeople who are now sales managers coach by mimicking

how they were managed and coached—more often than not with a heavy, outdated push style."[16] Furthermore, sales coaches who were top performers often don't know exactly *why* they were successful as salespeople, so they can't effectively impart what they know to others. (See also Sales Trap 21, "Top Performers Are the Best Teachers.") You can't share the secrets of your success if you aren't quite sure what they are! Even when managers are able to pass along their knowledge effectively, that knowledge is often outdated and therefore no longer applicable.

Many sales managers haven't even taken their own company's sales training program, whereas the sales staff have. The reason for this is that when a company changes its basic skill training program, the sales managers who learned the old program never have time to take the new one. Management wonders, Why should our sales managers take this course? They don't need training. They can sell. However, while they may not need to take the sales training program to improve their own performance, they need to be able to reinforce their salespeople who have taken the new program using the labels and language from that program. Top companies have a common language, which is reinforced through training. Admittedly, this can be expensive if you continually change training programs.

MANAGERS LACK COACHING SKILLS

Sales-skill coaching is a specialized skill, different from sales management. Sales managers are often simply not trained by their companies to coach selling skills, so they don't know how. Salespeople complain that the coaching they receive is too basic to help them meet their customers' escalating demands.[17] The critical coaching skill that sales managers usually lack is giving effective feedback and reinforcement.[18]

MANAGERS AREN'T GIVEN INCENTIVES TO COACH

Companies rarely reward managers for coaching (with incentives such as compensation, promotion, good performance reviews, or simple recognition). When was the last time you attended a recognition or award meeting at which a manager was recognized with a plaque for his or her development of people?

Marion Miller, a thirty-year veteran with Xerox in sales, sales management, and human resources, had this to say:

> We are committed to developing our people at Xerox. We train them extensively, we have one of the best training programs in the world, we include people development in management reviews, and we genuinely care about our people, but I can't remember when we have recognized a manager solely for the development of his or her people.

ACTION POINTS

→ *Salespeople need coaching in order to learn.* Companies that want to see a financial return on their training costs and want to see their salespeople improve need to either train sales managers to coach or subcontract coaching outside the company.

→ *Reward sales managers for coaching.* It's good to include monetary incentives and to devote a section of annual review to their effectiveness in developing their people, and it is even better to send a message throughout an organization that says: "We do care about our people. We want to recognize those who are responsible for the development of our people—people who develop the best in others. We want to recognize and reward them in public and at departmentwide, divisionwide, or companywide meetings."

→ *Salespeople should take responsibility.* No one else can take responsibility for a salesperson's performance. You must take the ultimate responsibility for your own development. A company can give you extensive opportunities to grow and improve—providing books, materials, training classes, and mentoring—but in the end, you are the one who decides how much effort you will put into your development.

SALES TRUTH 22: Sales managers usually *aren't* good coaches.

PRINCIPLE

use the internet

TOP PERFORMERS and top companies use the Internet effectively to enhance their sales efforts. They recognize that the Internet can be a customer acquisition tool, a low-cost distribution channel, and a lead generator. Internet technology and its uses are dynamic, limited only by the creativity of the sales and marketing people using them. Top companies are constantly figuring out how to use online selling as an effective tool.

One clever sales use of the Internet is Dell's Premier Pages. Premier Pages are customized web sites that Dell offers free of charge to corporations, governments, and institutions. Dell's Premier Pages offer secure, personalized web sites that provide:

△ Order history

△ Order status

△ Contact information for Dell account teams

△ Troubleshooting services

△ Product specifications

Dell claims to have more than 40,000 Premier Pages being accessed by customers in as many as twelve languages.[1] Dell uses this free web service to entice potential customers when salespeople are making sales calls. "We use these as an acquisition tool—we can have them up in less than 24 hours," says Chris Hinkle, manager of Dell Latin America Online in Round Rock, Texas. "These are especially important for multinationals with offices around the world."[2]

Overall, the effect of the Internet is to transfer low-value sales functions to virtual networks because these networks are cheaper than a direct sales force. This has meant a reduction in field sales forces, but it hasn't replaced consultative salespeople. Consultative salespeople are still needed for important, high-value activities (such as getting new business, negotiating complicated pricing structures, and other key major account tasks).

Sales organizations that want to succeed today—let alone in the future—must figure out how to use technology to give them a leading edge over their competitors in order to create customer value.

WEB-BASED PRESENCE

Of course, top performers have long recognized the importance of technology (both hardware and software) in managing databases and prospect lists effectively, as well as for communicating by e-mail.

Today, those functions are all in the ever-present laptop, which now also has wireless Internet access. Some sales organizations use laptops extensively. As one advertisement suggests, they "don't leave home without it." Salespeople at these organizations, such as Oracle, IBM, Xerox, and Hewlett-Packard, not only swap e-mails with their clients, but also perform tasks such as inputting orders, updating databases and forecasts, drafting proposals, and accessing information, all the while being connected to their company's central computer. Salespeople also use such tools to do their homework and research prospective customers before the sales call. (See also Sales Trap 18, "A Skilled Salesperson Doesn't Need to Plan Sales Calls.")

E-MAIL

Is e-mail too impersonal a mode of communication for consultative salespeople to use to advance the sale and to develop meaningful customer relationships? Opinions abound. On the one hand, a strong sales personality we know says, "My customers want to press flesh, not keys."

But there are a growing number of consultants and salespeople who disagree. One colleague at The Dartmouth Group, Ltd., who heads up operations in the high-tech market, believes that while it's important to hold face-to-face meetings, these meetings can be combined with e-mail when developing relationships. He cautions against downplaying the usefulness of e-mail to build and solidify relationships.

According to this source, e-mail is a two-edged sword. On the downside, because clients may receive up to 100 e-mails a day, they often don't take the time to respond to each one. "On the upside, however, e-mail provides people an opportunity to respond, document, and offer pensive answers to thoughtful queries," he claims. "The key to e-mail is constructing concise, high-impact statements and asking thoughtful questions that almost come across as 'thirty-second sound bites' to the other party. Respect for one another can result if both parties use e-mail effectively." Naturally, effective writing skills are important to making e-mail work. As Jeffrey Gitomer, author of *The Sales Bible*, says, "Writing skills, grammar, humor, and prose are integral in showing customers how sales-intelligent you are."[3]

Whether through web sites or web-based technologies such as e-mail, the Internet is transforming the way companies buy and sell and the way the sales consulting professions communicate. But companies should be aware of the sales traps that prevent the effective use of the Internet.

*　　*　　*

> ## sales trap 23:
> # The Internet Has Changed Selling

People say that the Internet has changed selling. The Internet may have opened up new venues for selling, but it's actually just another form of direct marketing. In moving selling online, the Internet has opened up new sales opportunities and added new roles for buyers and sellers. It has also changed buying patterns, giving customers more choices. Despite these changes, virtual sales are still just transactional sales.

CHANGES IN SELLING

Business-to-business (B2B) e-commerce has changed the way businesses work with their accounts by offering new ways for accounts to connect with service providers (or manufacturers), and new ways for service providers (or manufacturers) to connect with their suppliers. B2B e-commerce shifts low-value sales to virtual channels because these channels are automated and electronic and are therefore more efficient and cheaper than personal selling. It is difficult to create value in these sales (Sales Traps 11 and 12), and the customer's primary decision criterion is price.

One way sellers use the Internet to foster loyalty, boost sales, and cut costs is by using web-based extranets for major accounts. Cleveland-based Applied Industrial Technologies, Inc., added private extranets for customers. The problem that this $1.5 billion (1998) industrial parts distributor had faced was that customers had difficulty choosing from among its thousands upon thousands of different industrial parts. Selling was hard to coordinate for its 900 field salespeople and 1,400 inside salespeople because each customer had individual price agreements determined by geography, sales volume, and corporate negotiations. Therefore, a simple web catalog for all visitors wouldn't be appropriate.[4] A private extranet for each customer was the solution. An extranet is a para-enterprise network that organizations use to extend intranets to existing outside customers and suppliers. Applied Industrial Technologies' extranet:

△ Shows the prices for the individual company

△ Allows customers to purchase products

△ Allows customers to check the inventory of local branches in real time

△ Allows customers to review orders from the past two years[5]

The extranets increase efficiency. "They allow us to be more efficient, and therefore more profitable," says John Dannemiller, chairman and CEO of Applied Industrial Technologies, Inc. The extranets are also expected to allow the company to open its market to smaller accounts, whose small purchases wouldn't make a sales call by a field rep profitable.[6] Interestingly, however, new customers have to go through a local branch and salesperson first. Prospects have the alternative of filling out a form on the site, which is sent to the appropriate local branch within twenty-four hours. Salespeople are expected to contact the customer within a few days.[7]

CHANGES IN BUYING

B2B commerce on the Internet has opened up opportunities for buyers, too, allowing them access to purchasing opportunities they didn't have in the past. Procurement processing inefficiencies are eliminated because automation is substituted for manual processing of forms. Buyers are able to find the best price, product information, and resources that are in short or excess supply faster and more easily.

One way in which B2B e-commerce benefits buyers is by giving them access to markets they wouldn't have access to otherwise. For example, buyers in the paper market, traditionally a highly fragmented market in which over 500 printers buy paper from a few giant paper manufacturers, can now take advantage of online web exchanges, such as PaperExchange.com. An exchange is an impartial site that collects quotes from sellers and submits them to buyers, and vice versa. For example, in what is called a reverse auction, a buyer can post a particular material it needs and cite the price it is willing to pay and the product specifications it needs (delivery, size, time, amount, etc.). Suppliers can then give a quote online.[8] PlasticsNet.com, owned by Chicago-based Commerx, Inc., is another example of an exchange; it offers buyers in the plastics market access to raw and manufactured materials through online auctions.[9]

The Internet increases efficiency, giving buyers the chance to purchase material that is in excess supply. In the paper industry, to recover high fixed costs, huge paper mills must run continuously. If paper demand ebbs, inventory soars. In the past, the manufacturers had to employ large and costly sales forces to move the excess inventory. But field sales forces could profitably call on only bigger accounts. Today, there's a virtual marketplace of buyers that the mill's sales reps might never have been able to contact.

OLD WINE IN A NEW BOTTLE

Although these changes are changes in ways of buying and selling, it's important to remember that in the larger scheme of things, they're still plain-vanilla transactional sales. And transactional sales have been around for a long time. It's hard to imagine consultative sales taking place on the Internet.[10] (For a discussion of whether the Internet will replace consultative salespeople, see Sales Trap 24.)

Selling and buying on the Internet is just another form of direct marketing. As Michael Dell himself has said, initially, in 1994, he viewed the Internet as just another way to sell direct, a tool that would strengthen Dell in its primary mission to be a one-on-one, direct-to-the-consumer computer company. "Direct from Dell" pioneered computers as a direct sale with no intermediaries. Dell pioneered the strategy that instead of a catalog and a telephone customer service number, customers used the Dell.com web site. "It's self-service," Michael Dell says. "The customer is now going [to the web site], and they're not calling us on the phone."[11]

Others agree. "Direct marketers are the only true beneficiaries of the Internet," states Lester Wunderman, one of the pioneers of direct marketing.[12] Internet selling and buying relies on the same sales processes, principles, and techniques as other forms of direct transactional sales. (The techniques in transactional sales are discussed in Sales Trap 20, "If You Generate Sales Activity, You'll Close More Sales.")

With respect to selling, the Internet is old wine in a new bottle. Although it's a new technology, Internet sales are transactional direct sales, and direct sales are as old as money. However, the impact of the technology has changed both selling and buying patterns. It doesn't change *why* companies buy and sell, but it changes what, when, where, and how companies buy and sell.

ACTION POINTS

→ *Use the Internet to buy and sell direct.* The Internet is a transactional selling tool that is used to buy and sell direct. Period. Using the Internet to sell increases your profitability on low-margin product lines by taking the direct sales expense for salespeople out of the P&L statement.

→ *Survey the market.* What are your competitors doing online?

→ *Survey your customers.* What information and services will your customers want from your site twelve months from now? How do they want to use the Internet to stay in touch with you?

→ *Use the Internet as a channel of distribution for low-value products.*
Allow your customers to use the Internet to buy certain lines of
products for which sales reps will provide little or no value to
customers.

→ *Use the Internet to offer your customers more choices and more information.* The Internet offers sellers a cheaper way to reach and
inform customers than communication methods in the past.

**SALES TRUTH 23: The internet is just another
venue for transactional sales.**

---

sales trap 24:
The Internet Will Replace All Consultative Salespeople

Although the Internet has replaced some consultative salespeople, it will never replace them all. Many of the low-value sales functions in business-to-business (B2B) selling that were formerly handled by consultative salespeople have now been shifted to online sales. The transactions shifted to the Web include those related to:

△ Routine purchases

△ Product information

△ Discount information

△ Pricing information

△ Contact information for account teams

△ Smaller accounts

△ Existing accounts

△ Researching products

△ Placing orders (for existing customers)

△ Checking on the status of orders

As Bill Gates says, "As the Internet drives down the cost of transactions, the middlemen will disappear or evolve to add new value."[13] One sales recruiter said that his company uses a combination of inside salespeople (outbound and inbound telemarketing) and the Internet to sell computer hardware and software equipment to its customers. By doing this, the company doesn't incur the costs associated with an outside sales force. One might argue that with the sophistication of call centers, the Internet and web sites, field sales organization must discover new ways to create value for their customers in order to justify their existence. The Internet may be responsible for sales force reductions of between 35 to 40 percent by 2005.[14]

Tim Furey is CEO of Oxford Associates, Inc., a sales consultancy firm in Bethesda, Maryland, and coauthor of *The Channel Advantage*.[15] He says:

> The Internet has clearly cut field sales forces and has moved many previously face-to-face functions online or in-house. But the consultative salesperson will remain. Most of the hype around the Internet—the Amazon.coms, the eBays—[is] around relatively simple, off-the-rack, commodity products that can be sold with minimal human involvement.

Getting a customer to sign a two-year, multimillion-dollar industrial parts contract probably won't happen online. The transactions that are staying with consultative salespeople include those relating to:

Δ Acquiring new business

Δ Negotiating individual pricing agreements

Δ Negotiating configuration exceptions

Δ Customizing solutions

Δ Resolving complicated issues, services, and products

Δ Handling major accounts

Δ Managing situations in which the sales consultant has to create value, i.e., situations that are too qualitative without his or her involvement

In the future, there may be fewer consultative salespeople. Those that remain will have to be sure that they add value. Principle 4, "Create Value," and Sales Traps 9 through 18 in that section will remain as true tomorrow as they are today.

B2B E-COMMERCE

The majority of e-commerce transactions are B2B, where most consultative selling has traditionally taken place. This more than anything else probably accounts for the decline in consultative sales positions. Forrester Research, Inc., reports that in 1998, B2B e-commerce accounted for $43 billion in transactions, compared to $7.8 billion in business-to-consumer (B2C) transactions.[16] The computer industry claims the largest percentage of online B2B sales transactions; these transactions were valued at $50.4 billion (45 percent of online transactions) in 1999.[17] And Forrester estimates that the online B2B market will grow to $1.3 trillion by 2003.[18] Goldman Sachs estimates sales in B2B e-commerce by 2004 of:

Δ Chemicals, $349 billion

Δ Computer hardware and software, $221 billion

Δ Industrial equipment, $140 billion

Δ Energy/utilities, $133 billion[19]

Because of this expected growth in online sales, the number of consultative sales positions is expected to continue to be reduced, but these positions will not be eliminated.

ONLINE SELLING. B2B e-commerce increasingly uses web-based sites and extranets (para-enterprise network organizations that extend intranets to existing outside customers and suppliers) for online selling. Much of this selling is automated and directed by the customers themselves. Larry Carter, CFO of Cisco Systems, even claims that

55 percent of orders pass through Cisco's system without being touched by anyone.[20]

NEW CUSTOMERS. Despite these changes, many companies still refer online sales from new customers to a salesperson. Cisco may have had $9.5 billion in online sales in 1999, more than three-quarters of its total sales for the year, but if you try to order from Cisco and you haven't set up an account through a dealer, you can't do it. New customers have to register with a dealer before they can purchase online.[21] And Cisco is not alone in this. A recent study by Shelley Taylor & Associates found that 90 out of 100 web sites (from the 1,000 largest companies in the world) sold products to other businesses, but only 9 allowed new customers to initiate a sale online.[22] Many people don't realize that companies are focusing their B2B efforts not on acquiring new customers, but on converting current customers to web-based ordering, sales, and customer service.[23] The high-value activity of acquiring new business is still left for consultative salespeople.

REDUCTIONS IN SALES COSTS AND SALES FORCES. There is evidence that sales expenses have declined and sales productivity has increased since sales have moved online. For example, Cisco Systems, which sells about 80 percent of the routers and other forms of networking gear that power the Internet, now handles 80 percent of its orders online. Cisco Systems sold an estimated $15 billion online in 2000.[24] Larry Carter, CFO of Cisco Systems, reports that in 1999, Cisco's networked business model saved over $800 million, while increasing salespeople's productivity by 15 percent.[25] While 80 percent of Cisco's orders are online, the other 20 percent involve higher-value sales activities carried out by internal and external salespeople (remember the 80/20 rule).

Dell has also lowered its sales expenses using the Internet. For example, Dell Computer's U.S. web site, which was launched in July of 1996, sells $40 million a day and accounts for 50 percent of Dell's

U.S. sales.[26] Dell allows customers to initiate orders online, but always follows up an online order with a call from a customer service person.[27] Salespeople get credit for online orders when customers write in the name of their salesperson, and regional marketing managers set online revenue goals for the sales team.[28] The Internet has helped Dell lower its sales, general, and administrative expenses from 15 percent of its revenues in fiscal year 1994 to 9.4 percent in 2000. Michael Dell believes that further reductions in these costs are still possible, even as much as half again.[29]

Several leading companies have virtually eliminated their sales forces in favor of independent solution providers. Microsoft and Dell are just two examples. Other companies have reduced their field sales forces and chosen to go with distributors, dealers, and value-added resellers. After exploring alternative channels for years in order to reduce sales overhead and be more price-competitive, IBM and Xerox have both turned to independent solution providers.

A final note: As I look around, I see fewer road warriors on planes than I used to. Companies have gotten smarter and are using fewer outside field salespeople. The message seems to be that companies are looking for a few good field sales representatives to call on their clients. Like the Marines, a few good people are left with getting the job done on the outside. The salesperson and consultative marketer of tomorrow will have to be really good at what she or he does, since the competition will be so fierce for fewer jobs.

ACTION POINTS

→ *Expect further reductions in sales forces.* The Internet is expected to continue to reduce the number of sales representatives and change the ways in which businesses sell to each other. As sales expenses decrease and the Internet continues to grow, employment in direct sales forces is expected to continue to decrease. Sales organizations should plan on reducing cost of sales by opting for inside sales reps.

→ *Consider team selling with higher-potential accounts.* Many of the *Fortune* 500 companies approach particular industries (education, insurance, utilities, etc.) and high-potential accounts with sales teams that include not only a manager from the sales department but also managers and representatives from engineering, service, and research and development. Such team sales efforts bring strengths from many functional areas to bear on the account. Procter & Gamble and IBM are two examples of companies that have used this team sales approach successfully. According to Jill Summers, a former Procter & Gamble manager who is now with Eli Lilly, "We have vice presidents who often head up our customer teams who call on our larger accounts, such as Wal-Mart."

SALES TRUTH 24: Consultative salespeople will remain, but in reduced numbers.

the next generation of performance change programs

AT THE beginning of this book, I stated that I would begin with the end in mind. We are at the end. But, is it really the end? Yes, it is the end of this book, but it is not the end of the sales profession's attempt to discover different solutions and new perspectives to improve their performance results in their chosen field. This quest will probably never end. Whenever you insert the variable of people, in this case salespeople, into an equation, the answers are never absolute. However, there will probably always be the quest to figure out this

Rubik's Cube of sales. And don't think people aren't working real hard at it. But how do we answer this most important question: How can we further optimize individual sales performance's above the levels we have already achieved with the world's finest performance change programs?

This book has taken a "best practices" approach to improving sales results. It has identified 24 sales traps, based upon thoughtful research, that top performers are likely to avoid. So, what is wrong with focusing on these 24 sales traps and becoming a sales star? Aren't they the "best practices" that you need to process and execute for stardom? Well, yes, but they are missing the same key ingredient that sales training programs of today—the first generation—are missing. These "best practices" approaches must be customized to the sales consultant's customer organization at an entirely new level if they are to ultimately achieve performance change and therefore improved results for the salesperson and his or her company. Therefore, a second generation of training utilizing a higher-level, customized approach to performance change will most likely emerge.

To put it another way, the value proposition will be different in this new millennium. Salespeople will not just be delivering the same value proposition in a different way. For example, today the most effective training programs use some type of sales model that needs to be learned in order to bring about a change in individual and group performance. Some of these models are well researched and formulated; others are overly complex, difficult to learn, and not correlated with top performance. All these models, however, have one thing in common: *They are totally free of business knowledge.* They are simply generic frameworks. In other words, "We will teach you our sales models, then you need to figure out how to translate them to *your* real world."

For example, it's not about learning the finer points of some probing model for asking questions—it's about learning the questions that bring business results in the buying scenarios that represent the customer's marketplace. More specifically, how can a salesperson ask really smart questions if she or he doesn't really know the customer and the customer's marketplace? She or he can't. That's business knowledge. The content of tomorrow's generation of programs needs to address this knowledge issue through its content and its facilitators.

In summary, the major topic areas for improving sales results are not unique. The research clearly indicates which core skills make top performers. When it comes to face-to-face customer interactions, salespeople need to avoid the 24 sales traps. So, where are we headed?

Dr. Richard Ruff, president of Sales Momentum in Scottsdale, Arizona, and coauthor of *Getting Partnering Right and Managing Major Sales*, strongly believes that the next step in achieving performance change and improving sales results will involve customizing programs to a second generation of standards using a "best practices" approach as the core strategies and skills.

According to Ruff:

> There are two unique points that should strongly be considered when figuring out how to move sales performance and sales results to the next level. First, performance change programs must incorporate a customer survey that is customized for the program, and performance change programs should also examine the success factors from the customer's perspective. Second, the program must incorporate into each case study the "best practices" of your top salespeople. In other words, we must leverage the insights of an organization's best people in order to help others within the company.

So, as I end this book, I can't help but wonder what a third generation of performance change might look like. The good news? I don't have to worry about it until the second generation grows up and comes of age. Good luck, and may all of you become value creators!

Dick Canada
Hanover, New Hampshire
August, 2001

Contact: Dick Canada
E-Mail: rcanada@indiana.edu
Kelley School of Business
Indiana University
Bloomington, IN 47405
812-855-8878

    or

The Institute for Global Sales Studies
Kelley School of Business
Indiana University
www.bus.indiana.edu/globalsales

    or

The Dartmouth Group, Ltd.
10333 N. Meridian Street, Ste. 230
Indianapolis, IN 46290
317-573-4844
www.dartmouthgroup.com

notes

NOTE FOR PREFACE

1. Neil Rackham conducted the study at Xerox. Rackham is a preeminent sales researcher who studied 35,000 sales calls in 23 countries over a period of 12 years. He is the author of over fifty research and technical papers, and his works have been translated into thirteen languages.

NOTES FOR CHAPTER 1

1. Conversation with the author.

2. Conversations between the author and Neil Rackham during August 2000.

3. Jamie Comstock and Garry Higgins, "Appropriate Relational Messages in Direct Selling Interaction: Should Salespeople Adapt to Buyers' Communicator Style?" *Journal of Business Communication*, 34, no. 4 (1990): 401–418. Comstock and Higgins studied 100 advertising buyers from 100 different companies in a medium-sized city in the Florida panhandle. Participants were selected to provide a proportional representation of businesses within the community. Buyers were predominantly male (67 percent) and Anglo (79 percent). Observations by The Dartmouth Group, Ltd., and conversations with the Indiana University Institute for Sales Studies confirm Comstock and Higgins's findings.

4. Ibid.

5. Ibid.

6. The Dartmouth Group, Ltd., field observations of salespeople who "give information versus seek information" and their resulting success on sales calls.

7. Robert B. Miller and Stephen E. Heiman with Tad Tuleja, *Strategic Selling* (New York: Warner Books, 1986) and Neil Rackham's study of 35,000 sales calls in 23 countries over a period of 12 years. Miller and Heiman and Rackham diverge on the specific characteristics of coaches, but both emphasize their importance.

8. Miller and Heiman, *Strategic Selling*, chap. 12, "Your Coach: A Key to the Other Buying Influences," 208–213.

9. Miller and Heiman argue that the coach can be found anywhere: in your organization, in the buying organization, or outside both. In *Strategic Selling* they discuss the criteria for a good coach on pp. 83–87. They define the coach's role as "to provide information, direction, guidance—and in many cases access to the other Buying Influences. *But the Coach doesn't do your selling for you* [emphasis theirs]" (215–216).

10. Miller and Heiman, *Strategic Selling*.

11. Stephen E. Heiman and Diane Sanchez with Tad Tuleja, *The New Conceptual Selling* (New York: Warner Books, 1999), Neil Rackham, *SPIN® Selling* (New York: McGraw-Hill, 1988), and Achieve-Global, *Professional Selling Skills IV,* further support this point.

12. Neil Rackham's study of 35,000 sales calls in 23 countries over a period of 12 years, cited in *SPIN® Selling*, 61.

13. Neil Rackham and John Carlisle, "The Effective Negotiator— Part I: The Behavior of Successful Negotiators," *Journal of European Industrial Design Training 2*, no. 6 (1978): 6–11.

NOTES FOR CHAPTER 2

1. *POOPS Matrix* for September 7, 2000 through September 28, 2000, Undergraduate Career Services, Kelley School of Business, Indiana University, Bloomington, IN 47405.

2. National Collegiate Sales Competition (NCSC) Event, Baylor University, Center for Professional Selling, Waco, TX 76798, February 25–26, 2000. Baylor University Center for Professional Selling, National Collegiate Sales Competition (NCSC) Event, P.O. Box 98007, Waco, TX, 76798, telephone 254-710-4246.

3. Conversation between the author and Jonathan Walsman, former account manager, Xerox Corporation, Indianapolis, IN, June 26, 2000.

4. Argyris and Schon first proposed double-loop learning theory in C. Argyris and D. Schon, *Increasing Leadership Effectiveness* (San Francisco: Jossey-Bass, 1976). Double-loop learning is a theory of personal change, or how an individual learns to change underlying values and assumptions. Double-loop learning incorporates "theory of action," a perspective first outlined by Argyris & Schon in *Theory in Practice* (San Francisco: Jossey-Bass, 1974). "Theory of action" (or what people think they do) takes the perspective that human beings are actors and that an individual's behavior is part of and is informed by his or her theory of action.

An important contrast to the theory of action is an individual's "theory-in-use" (what people *actually* do, as opposed to what they *think* they do). Bringing what people think they do (theory of action) and what they actually do (theory-in-use) into congruence is a primary concern of double-loop learning. Typically, interaction with others is necessary in order to identify the conflict between the two.

There are four basic steps in applying action theory: (1) discovery of the espoused theory of action and actual theory-in-use, (2) the invention of new meanings for each, (3) the production of new actions, and (4) generalization of results.

In double-loop learning, assumptions underlying current views are questioned and hypotheses about behavior are tested publicly. The end result should be increased effectiveness in decision making and better acceptance of failures and mistakes.

See *www.hfni.gsehd.gwu.edu/~tip/argyris.html*

5. The Dartmouth Group, Ltd., ten-year field studies of sales top performers.

6. "Sales U? Companies Want Graduates Who Can Sell Now," *The Wall Street Journal*, October 12, 1999, A-1.

7. Conversations between Neil Rackham and the author.

8. Rosann L. Spiro and Barton Weitz, "Adaptive Selling: Conceptualization, Measurement and Nomological Validity," *Journal of Marketing Research*, February 1990. Dr. Spiro is also a coauthor of a best-selling sales management textbook, William J. Stanton, Rosann Spiro, and Richard Buskirk, *Management of a Sales Force*, 9th ed. (Homewood, IL: Irwin, 1995), which also cites her and Dr. Weitz's original study (p. 252). Dr. Weitz is also coauthor with Stephen B. Castleberry and John F. Tanner, Jr., of the college textbook *Selling: Building Partnerships*, 3d ed. (New York: Irwin/McGraw-Hill, 1998).

9. Rackham's studies, later published in *SPIN® Selling* (New York: McGraw-Hill, 1988), debunked this myth. He discovered that whether a question was open or closed wasn't as important as the type of question within each category.

10. "Sales U?" A-1 and class syllabi submitted at the American Marketing Association Nineteenth Annual Faculty Consortium on Professional Selling and Sales Management, Orlando, Florida, July 1999.

11. Presentation by Jon Hawes, Director, Fisher Institute for Professional Selling at the University of Akron, at the American Marketing Association Nineteenth Annual Faculty Consortium on Professional Selling and Sales Management, Orlando, Florida, July 1999. The University of Akron also offers a minor (18 credits) and a certificate (15 credits) in sales.

12. Selected colleges and universities are from "Sales U?" A-1 and class syllabi submitted at the American Marketing Association Nineteenth Annual Faculty Consortium on Professional Selling and Sales Management, Orlando, Florida, July 1999.

13. "Sales U?" A-1.

14. Ibid.

15. William J. Stanton, Rosann Spiro, and Richard Buskirk, *Management of a Sales Force*, 9th ed. (Homewood, IL: Irwin, 1995). Also, The Dartmouth Group, Ltd., ten-year field studies of top performers. Top performers tended to have solid interpersonal skills, but there didn't seem to be an initial correlation between investigative skills and interpersonal skills or adaptive skills, leading us to conclude that selling skills needed to be developed, i.e., people were not born with them. Although the observations by the Dartmouth Group, Ltd., were field observations and not formal studies, this inference meets the test of reasonableness.

16. Observations by the Dartmouth Group, Ltd., personnel, including Mike Navel, Tricia Wilson, Mark Slaby, Susan Woods, and Gina Shupe.

17. Conversations between the author and Neil Rackham during August 2000.

NOTES FOR CHAPTER 3

1. Conversation between the author and Don Argay, Manager, Training & Development, Eli Lilly Pharmaceutical Division, 1993, at Eli Lilly corporate offices in Indianapolis, Indiana. Eli Lilly's sales organization called on physicians and used a customized sales program developed especially for Eli Lilly.

2. Sales researcher Neil Rackham found that strategically customized training programs were likely to be nearly twice as effective as off-the-shelf, generic programs. (IKON seminar in Atlanta, Georgia in October 1996.)

3. I joined Xerox in 1971, when its national training facility was located at the Sheraton Hotel in Ft. Lauderdale, Florida. In June of 1971, I participated in the first version (PSS-1) of this continually evolving program (which as of this writing is in its fourth revision). In the mid-1970s, when I became a sales manager, I began teaching PSS to Xerox's new hires.

4. In research conducted by Neil Rackham in 1984–1985, even people who were well trained in communication style techniques couldn't identify the buyer's style when they watched videos of real sales calls.

5. One study, however showed no correlation between the seller's communication style and the style buyers said they prefer. Jamie Comstock and Garry Higgins, "Appropriate Relational Messages in Direct Selling Interaction: Should Salespeople Adapt to Buyer's Communicator Style?" *Journal of Business Communication* 34, no. 4 (1997): 401–418. Comstock and Higgins studied 100 advertising buyers from 100 different companies in a medium-sized city in the Florida panhandle. Participants were selected to provide a proportional representation of businesses within the community. Buyers were predominantly male (67 percent) and Anglo (79 percent).

6. Neil Rackham studied 35,000 sales calls in 23 countries over a period of 12 years and developed a behaviorally based program based on this research.

7. Neil Rackham's study at Xerox, cited in Neil Rackham and Richard Ruff, *Managing Major Sales* (New York, HarperBusiness, 1991), 128–130.

8. Interview between The Dartmouth Group, Ltd., personnel and the author in 1999.

NOTES FOR CHAPTER 4

1. Rackham's conclusion: "It's more important that your key ideas get to the decision-maker than that you should present them in person." Rackham's study of 35,000 sales calls in 23 countries over a period of 12 years is cited in his *Major Account Sales Strategy* (New York: McGraw-Hill, 1989), 19–20, 34.

2. The Dartmouth Group, Ltd., field study observations, 1995–1999.

3. Neil Rackham labels objective criteria as "hard" in *Major Account Sales Strategy*.

4. *www.salesdoctors.com/diagnosis/3value3.htm.*

5. The Dartmouth Group, Ltd., memorandum by Susan Woods dated December 9, 1998.

6. Ibid.

7. Tom Fee of Sales Process Solutions, Inc., "Their [customers'] responsibilities to themselves and their stakeholders (employees, stockholders, customers, etc.) have become their [customers'] overriding concern." *www.salesdoctors.com/diagnosis/3rel.htm*, fall 1999.

8. Lecture given by Neil Rackham during a sales management class at Indiana University on April 12, 2000.

9. Discussion with Dr. Richard Ruff in August 2000.

10. Neil Rackham, "Why Bad Things Happen to Good Products," *Journal of Product Innovation Management*, May 1998.

11. The Dartmouth Group, Ltd., behavioral analysis studies at the MEDSTAT Group, 1999–2000.

12. The phrase "don't let enthusiasm get in the way" is from conversations between the author and Neil Rackham during August 2000.

13. Neil Rackham's study of 35,000 sales calls in 23 countries over a period of 12 years, cited in Rackham, *Major Account Sales Strategy*, 116. When customers told salespeople that the reason the salespeople had lost the business was price, 64 percent of the time price wasn't the main reason. More important factors were the risks and penalties that the customer feared would come from buying from a particular vendor.

14. Conversations between the author and Dr. Richard Ruff during Dr. Ruff's visit to the Kelley School of Business at Indiana University, April 5–7, 2000, and Neil Rackham's study of 35,000 sales calls in 23 countries over a period of 12 years, cited in Rackham, *Major Account Sales Strategy*, 116.

15. Ibid.

16. Private conversations between Neil Rackham and the author during visits to the Institute for Global Sales Studies at the Kelley School of Business at Indiana University and Neil Rackham's study of 35,000 sales calls in 23 countries over a period of 12 years, cited in Rackham, *Major Account Sales Strategy*, 124.

17. Deep-seated concerns are also discussed in Stephen E. Heiman and Diane Sanchez with Tad Tuleja, *The New Conceptual Selling* (New York: Warner Books, 1999); Neil Rackham, *SPIN® Selling* (New York: McGraw-Hill, 1988); and Kevin Davis and Kenneth H. Blanchard, *Getting Into Your Customer's Head: The Eight Roles of Customer Focused Selling* (New York: Times Books, 1996).

18. Strategic Marketing Class, August 1991 at Amos Tuck School of Business Administration at Dartmouth College.

19. The Dartmouth Group, Ltd., ten-year field observations of top performers, 1990–2000.

20. Conversations between the author and Neil Rackham in August 2000.

21. Ibid.

22. Ibid.

23. Ibid.

24. Neil Rackham's talk to the M426 Sales Management Class at Indiana University, April 12, 2000.

25. Private conversations between the author and Neil Rackham during Rackham's visits to the Institute for Global Sales Studies at the Kelley School of Business at Indiana University, and Neil Rackham's study of 35,000 sales calls in 23 countries over a period of 12 years, cited in Rackham, *Major Account Sales Strategy*, 116.

26. The Dartmouth Group, Ltd., field studies of top performers include observations of sales calls across many industries, such as telecommunications, office products, office furniture, computer software, publishing, health care, financial services, and banking from 1990 through 2000. Our field behavioral studies have included industry leaders like Xerox, Westinghouse, Eli Lilly, McGraw-Hill, and Herman-Miller distributor reps. Our observations of top performers indicate that they offer solutions later in the sales call than average or subpar performers.

27. Rolf B. White, ed., *The Great Business Quotations* (New York, Dell, 1986), 131.

28. The Dartmouth Group, Ltd. observations during a behavioral analysis study with Union Federal Bank, conducted by Mike Navel and Tracey Welch in 1998–1999 with Union Federal Bank small business lenders.

29. Linda Richardson, *Stop Telling, Start Selling: How to Use Customer-Focused Dialogue to Close Sales* (New York: McGraw-Hill, 1997), and Stephen E. Heiman and Diane Sanchez with Tad Tuleja, *The New Conceptual Selling* (New York: Warner Books, 1999), 182: "Good questions can motivate and sustain your customer's interest, stimulate her thinking and modify her attitudes."

30. Conversations with Neil Rackham suggest that salespeople are more likely to ask lots of questions when they believe the purpose is to understand rather than persuade. Neil Rackham's study of 35,000 sales calls in 23 countries over a period of 12 years, cited in Neil Rackham, *The SPIN® Selling Field Workbook* (New York: McGraw-Hill, 1999), 169.

31. Thomas N. Ingram with Raymond W. Laforge and Charles H. Schwepker, Jr., *Sales Management: Analysis and Decision Making*, 3d ed., The Dryden Press Series in Marketing, (Orlando, FL: HBJ, 1997).

32. Wilson Learning and IKON Office Solutions, 1995, 9.

33. "Selling at the Speed of Change (as Business Changes, Salespeople Must Change)" *Sales & Marketing Management*, 151, no. 11 (1999): S22.

34. John F. Monoky, "7 Attributes of Successful Sellers," *Industrial Distribution* 83, no. 3 (1994): 58.

NOTES FOR CHAPTER 5

1. Sales-skill-based programs usually contain probing models and techniques for uncovering and developing client needs. In some cases, negotiation behaviors are taught in a company's basic sales training program, but normally these skill behaviors are covered later, in the advanced training modules.

2. The Dartmouth Group, Ltd., ten-year study included a multinational office products company, 1990–2000. Many of its managers were not sufficiently familiar with their company's basic sales skill program to effectively coach and reinforce it.

3. Neil Rackham's study at Xerox, cited in Neil Rackham and Richard Ruff, *Managing Major Sales*, (New York: Harperbusiness, 1991), 129–130.

4. Learning International, *Sales Coaching: The Key to Leading a High-Performance Team* (Stamford, Conn.: Learning International, 1994), 10. This covers research conducted among leading sales organizations worldwide between 1992 and 1994.

5. This notion was documented in Rackham and Ruff, *Managing Major Sales*.

6. Neil Rackham's study of 35,000 sales calls in 23 countries over a period of 12 years, cited in Rackham and Ruff, *Managing Major Sales*, 13–14.

7. For further details on this finding, refer to Neil Rackham, *SPIN® Selling* (McGraw-Hill, 1988).

8. The Dartmouth Group, Ltd., ten-year field studies of top performers (1990–2000). Also confirmed by the Institute for Global Sales Studies, Indiana University, "Role Play Effectiveness in M430 Professional Selling Classes; 1995–2000; Persuasion Exercises Between Sellers & Buyers." See also Stephen E. Heiman and Diane Sanchez with Tad Tuleja, *The New Conceptual Selling* (New York: Warner Books, 1999), 33.

9. The Dartmouth Group, Ltd., ten-year field studies of top performers. Also confirmed by the Institute for Global Sales Studies, Kelley School of Business, Indiana University, "Role Play Effectiveness in M430 Professional Selling Classes; 1995–2000; Persuasion Exercises Between Sellers & Buyers."

10. The Dartmouth Group, Ltd., ten-year field studies of top performers (1990–2000). Also confirmed by the Institute for Global

Sales Studies, Kelley School of Business, Indiana University, "Role Play Effectiveness in M430 Professional Selling Classes; 1995-2000; Persuasion Exercises Between Sellers & Buyers."

11. Neil Rackham's research on 35,000 sales calls in 23 countries over a period of 12 years, cited in Rackham, *SPIN® Selling*, 132–133.

12. Ibid., 33.

13. Learning International, *Sales Coaching*, 2. "[But] data gathered during our most recent research, conducted among leading sales organizations worldwide between 1992 and 1994, revealed an alarming finding: Few sales managers *do* any real coaching at all." The research was conducted by Learning International (now Achieve Global) among leading sales organizations worldwide between 1992 and 1994.

14. Ibid., 10: "Most participants could easily describe the *attributes* of a good coach—and, indeed, there was widespread agreement about what those attributes are. There was very little agreement, however, about the *process* the sales coach uses to be effective." 24: "In addition, most participants acknowledged that there's a large gap between what sales coaching should be and what it is."

15. Ibid., 24: "Many organizations do not consider sales coaching to be a separate sales management discipline; instead, the sales manager's own sales experience is thought to be an adequate source of sales wisdom, strategies for improvement, and motivation."

16. Ibid., 25: "The sales managers learned and applied selling strategies that worked in a marketplace that no longer exists. Often, their experience in that marketplace is not relevant when trying to help salespeople deal with today's sales challenges."

17. Ibid., 26: "Yet salespeople say the coaching they receive is still too basic to help them meet their customers' escalating demands."

18. Ibid., 27: "Salespeople agreed that support and encouragement are important but feel that constructive feedback on their skills and performance is equally critical."

NOTES FOR CHAPTER 6

1. Margaret McKegney, "Dell Adapts Well to Online Sales," *Advertising Age International*, May 2000, 26.

2. Ibid.

3. Jeffrey Gitomer, "Here's Proof E-Commerce Is a Winner," *Birmingham Business Journal*, March 17, 2000, 15.

4. Chad Kaydo, "You've Got Sales," *Sales and Marketing Management* 151, no. 10 (1999): 28.

5. Ibid.

6. Ibid. Applied began testing the customer extranets with 12 clients in March 1999 and opened them to all customers in June 1999. By August 1999, more than 100 clients had registered to use the service.

7. Ibid.

8. Russ Banham, "The B-to-B Virtual Bazaar," *Journal of Accountancy* 190, no. 1 (2000): 26.

9. Ibid. PlasticsNet.com also offer users access to raw and manufactured materials through online exchanges and online catalogs.

10. "Consultative sales benefit a great deal from a salesperson's intimate knowledge of a customer's specific operations, knowledge that would be hard to match or replace electronically." Neil Rackham and John De Vincentis, *Rethinking the Sales Force* (New York: McGraw-Hill, 1999), 120.

11. "Dell to Detroit: Get into Gear Online!" *The Wall Street Journal*, December 1, 1999, B4.

12. Publishing Trends Conference, New York, November 1999, quoted in *Publisher's Weekly*, November 29, 1999, 25.

13. Bill Gates, with Collins Hemingway, *Business @ the Speed of Thought, Using a Digital Nervous System* (Warner Books, 1999), 90.

14. "By some estimates, at least half of today's selling positions will be gone by 2004." *Harvard Management* Update 4, no. 1 (1999): 11, quoting Neil Rackham and John De Vincentis.

15. Kaydo, "You've Got Sales."

16. Ibid.

17. Ibid.

18. Alf Nucifora, "Are You Preparing for the E-Business Revolution?" *Business Journal* (Central New York), vol. 14, no. 6 (2000), 20.

19. Ibid.

20. Cisco@speed, *The Economist*, June 29, 1999, 12.

21. Kaydo, "You've Got Sales."

22. Ibid.

23. Ibid.

24. Cisco@speed, *The Economist*.

25. Kaydo, "You've Got Sales.

26. McKegney, "Dell Adapts Well to Online Sales."

27. Ibid.

28. Ibid.

29. Daniel Roth, "Dell's Big Act," *Fortune*, December 6, 1999, 152.

index

about the author

Dick Canada, Executive Director of the Institute for Global Studies at Indiana University, is recognized as one of the country's leading experts in the area of improving field sales force effectiveness and productivity.

Canada began his sales career with Procter & Gamble, then joined Xerox to become Manager of Training and Development at its international training center. After leaving Xerox, he founded The Dartmouth Group, Ltd., which specializes in sales research and the development of sales models to improve productivity for companies involved in high-level selling.

Canada is currently a full-time member of the marketing faculty at the Kelley School of Business, Indiana University, where he has taught for 16 years. He has received many awards for classroom facilitation, including IU's "Student Choice Award," which is presented to the top three professors at the university. He also pursued postgraduate studies at Indiana University and studied strategic marketing at the Tuck School of Business at Dartmouth College.